Table of C

Part 1: Introduction
- Why this book
- Is vanlife for you?

Part 2: Plan
- Choose your van
- Design the layout
- Design the electrical system
- Design the plumbing system
- Buy your van

Part 3: Get ready
- Get the right tools
- Order van-specific supplies
- Select a hardware store
- Plumbing: Know-How
- Electrical Wiring: Know-How
- Cutting Weird Shapes: Know-How

Part 4: Build your van in 21 days
- Day 1: Fan Installation
- Day 2: Solar Panels
- Day 3: Electrical Roughing
- Day 4: Wall Insulation
- Day 5: Shower Framing
- Day 6: Fresh Water Tank

- Day 7: Grey Water Tank
- Day 8: Plumbing - Part 1
- Day 9: Electrical System
- Day 10: Ceiling - Insulation & Framing
- Day 11: Hanging Cabinets
- Day 12: Shower Tray & Fan
- Day 13: Shower Wet Panels & Framing
- Day 14 - Plumbing - Part 2
- Day 15: Outdoor Shower
- Day 16: Bed Frame
- Day 17: Painting & Staining
- Day 18: Kitchen
- Day 19: Sofa
- Day 20: Storage & Floors
- Day 21: Finishes

Part 5: Conclusion
- Last note
- About us

Van Build by Ben and Georgia Raffi

www.thevanbook.com

All information in this book has been carefully researched for accuracy. However, the author and publisher make no warranty, express or implied, that the information contained herein is appropriate for every individual, situation, or purpose, and assumes no responsibility for errors or omissions. The reader assumes the risk and full responsibility for all actions, and the author will not be held responsible for any loss or damage, whether consequential, incidental, special or otherwise that may result from the information presented in this book.

© 2020 Benjamin Raffi

All rights reserved. No portion of this book may be reproduced in any form without permission from the publisher, except as permitted by U.S. copyright law. For permissions contact:

help@thevanbook.com

Cover by Benjamin Raffi.
Photography by Georgia and Benjamin Raffi
Images by Benjamin Raffi and Bunnings Australia.

Paperback ISBN: 9798666381151

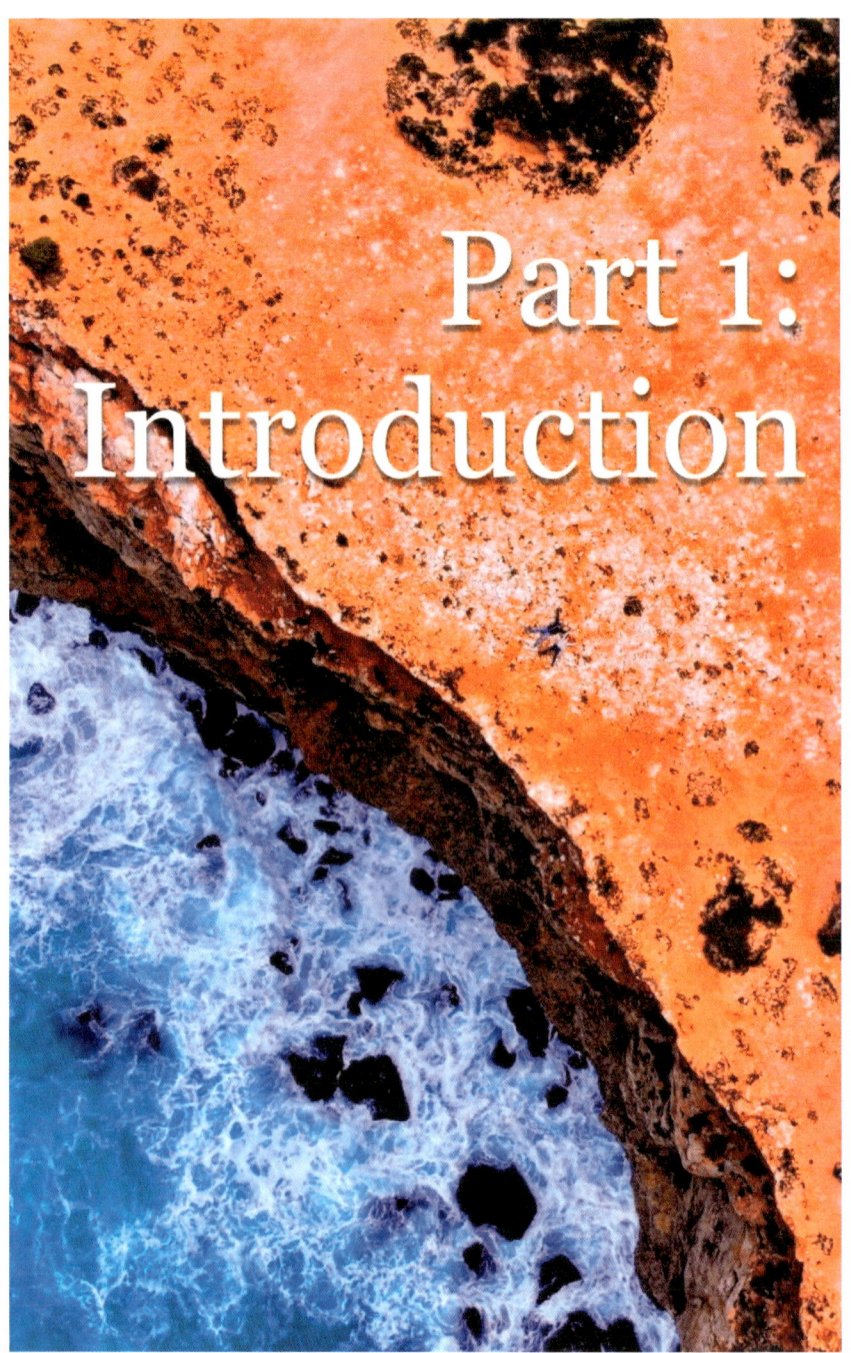

Why this book

Jumping into van life and living in a home on wheels is extremely exciting. Whether you want to have freedom to go to places less travelled, cut down on your expenses to give you the opportunity for a different career path, or meet awesome people, living on the road has a lot to offer.

However, many people don't know where to begin. Others are afraid that they'll have to give up comfort or modernity.

Our goal is to help more people take the jump and create a beautiful and comfortable home in a campervan or motorhome.

But why build your own campervan? First and foremost, because you'll be able to build it exactly the way you want it. And since it's such a small space, it's so much better to optimize the space for your needs. It's also a lot cheaper to build your van and you'll likely be able to sell it later for a profit. Finally, for us, it has been a way to gain new skills and use our bodies a lot more, having worked at desk jobs for over a decade.

This book will guide you through every step, from choosing a vehicle, to designing the layout, to plumbing and electrical systems, to self-building your new dream home — all in as little as 21 days, and with zero experience necessary.

Here's what you can expect from this book.

Step-by-step instructions.

We guide you each step of the way, with detailed descriptions and photos of our own build.

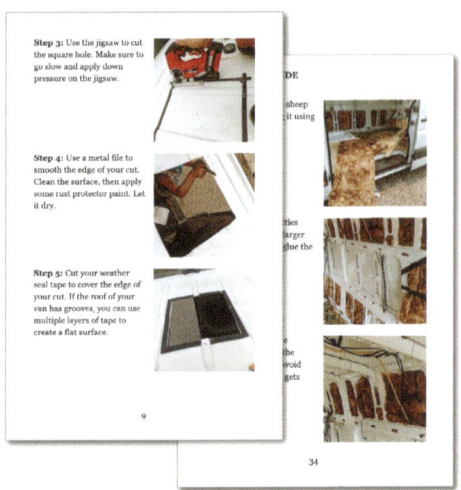

Detailed diagrams.

From electrical and plumbing systems to setting up your water tank or shower frame, our detailed diagrams will help you understand and master each part of the build.

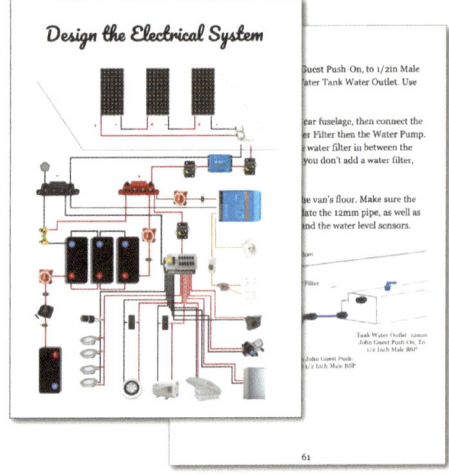

List of all supplies and tools.

For each step of the process, we detail all the tools and supplies you'll need. No matter which country you're building your van in, our lists will help you get everything you need, and know how to select the right tool for the job.

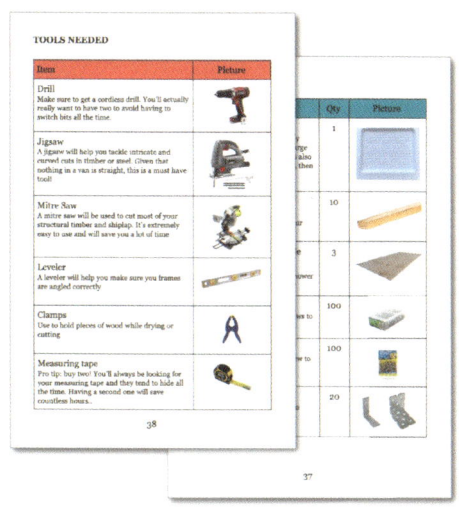

Tips & Know How.

From basic plumbing concepts, to tips on how to properly connect electrical wires, our tips and know-how sections help you master all the skills required to build your dream home.

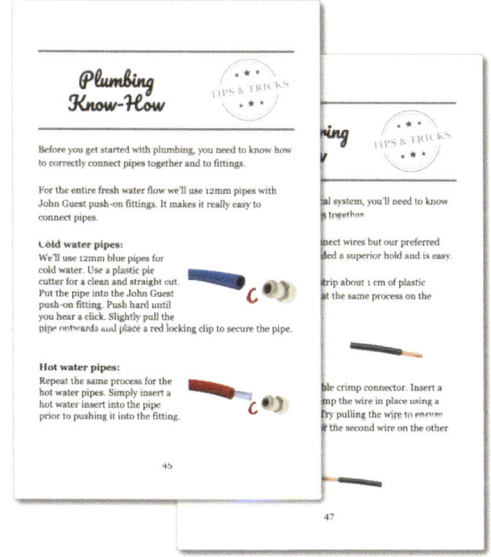

We've tried to make this book as detailed as possible, while keeping things simple. Instead of going into deep discussions about complex decisions - for example, whether you should wire your batteries in parallel or series - we will simply summarize what we know about it and what decisions we made based on extensive research. We've tried to save you time but if you'd like to be an expert on any of these topics, there is tons of information out there.

Is vanlife for you?

Living on the road, meeting other nomads, and discovering the world's most beautiful landscapes is amazing. However, this unconventional lifestyle isn't for everybody.

The most challenging aspect of this lifestyle is likely the amount of uncertainty. Most days, we travel to a new location, meet new people and try something new. And we absolutely love it. But, we have to be ok with not always knowing where we'll be sleeping or whether there will be a grocery store nearby. It requires a bit of planning, a bit of letting go, and replacing fears with curiosity. Of course there are nomads who plan their routes months in advance -- we just found that to be restrictive, and some of our best adventures are detours.

Another major aspect of vanlife is cost. A lot of people aren't sure if they can afford to take the leap. Well, there are many ways to make your dream come true and you don't necessarily need a ton of money. A few thousands dollars may be all you need to get your first van and build. You may need a bit of savings if you want a larger and more comfortable van -- but then, the cost of living on the road can actually be extremely cheap, and you may actually live rent free, and be able to sell your van after a few years for more than you purchased it. You'll need to be creative to continue making money on the road, but with increasing remote opportunities, it's absolutely doable.

A lot of people also ask us if we get lonely. Well, the truth is that we've never felt less lonely. Along our journey we often meet extraordinary people, a community of nomads, with incredibly diverse backgrounds and stories. And, we've been able to make instant connections with these people, sometimes building stronger bonds in hours than with people we had known for years.

What about living in a tiny space? Well, it's true that our new home is a lot smaller than other homes we've lived in. It's less spacious. It's more dusty. It's hard to have your "own" space. But it's also super cozy and it forces us to only keep things that we love and which make us happy. But the truth is, we're outdoors people. And living on the road allows us (or forces us) to spend a lot more time outdoors.

So, yes van life is amazing! Does it ever suck? Yes! When you get a cold, or it's raining for 5 days straight -- then you'd perhaps rather be in a proper home. But for us, it's so worth it.

Choose your van

One of the first steps you should think about is the type of vehicle you'd like to convert.

This decision is obviously one of the most important ones. It will depend on the number of people you plan to have living in the van, your budget, where you're planning on traveling, and how you want to travel.

A good place to start is figuring out how many people you'd like to accommodate in the van. Will you have an extra family member or friend crashing over from time to time? If so, you may want to have extra seating and a longer sofa for them to sleep on. Additionally, you'll need to decide if you want to be able to stand up in the van. For us, this was really important (and it makes it feel a lot more like a house).

Then, you'll need to figure out how much stuff you'll be bringing with you. Do you have a massive wardrobe you can't live without? For us, we have lots of outdoor "toys" -- from a small inflatable boat, to kitesurfs, spearguns, and more. So we needed to make sure everything would fit in the van.

Lastly, you'll want to consider how you plan to use your van. Will you be going off-grid for a long time? If so, you'll need bigger water tanks, a shower, a larger fridge, and so on. Will you be staying mostly in caravan parks or near cities? If so you can get by with much less.

We decided to go with a Mercedes Sprinter long wheelbase van. While Sprinter vans are a bit pricey, so is their resale value. They have a great reputation for lasting a long time -- especially those with diesel engines. The long wheelbase version is also tall enough for us to stand and long enough to fit a shower, a full queen size bed, and lots of storage.

There are many other great options, depending on your budget and needs. But, before you purchase your van, we recommend designing the layout of the interior to make sure everything will fit.

Design the layout

Now that you've selected a campervan model, you can design the layout of the interior of the van. You don't need to have all the decisions made (like what type of fridge you'd like) to get started.

First, we recommend doing some research and getting some inspiration using instagram or pinterest.

Here are some examples of Instagram accounts we found, that offer great inspiration:

	@vanliferules		@vanclans
	@vanlifecaptain		@camper_culture
	@vanlifedistrict		@camper_vancation

	@vanlife.living		@vanlife.goal
	@vanlifeisawesome		@van_boy_life
	@project.vanlife		@vanlifevirals
	@sprintercampervans		@vanlifetravelhub
	@lifeinsidcavan		@vanlifeclan
	@livingvanlife		@campervaninspo
	@packthevan		@homeiswhereyouparkit

Once you're inspired and have a better idea of what would work for you, search online or in dealership materials for the interior dimensions of your van model.

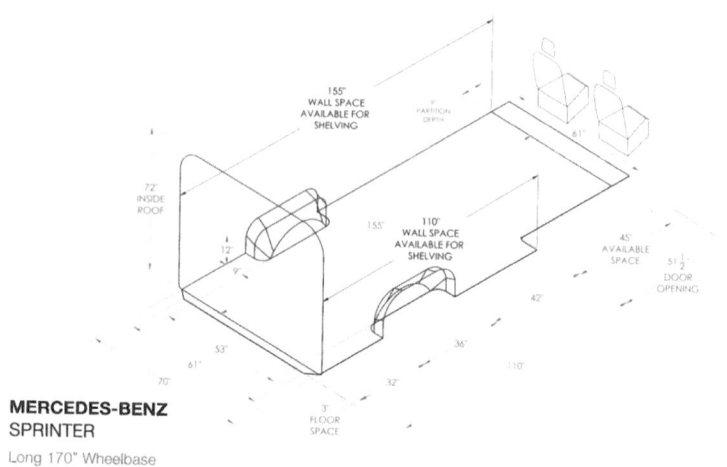

Then, we'd recommend drawing your dream layout using pen and paper. You can also use a software, such as SketchUp, but that will take a lot more time.

Here is one of the final drawings of the layout we imagined. (We ended up building almost the exact layout)

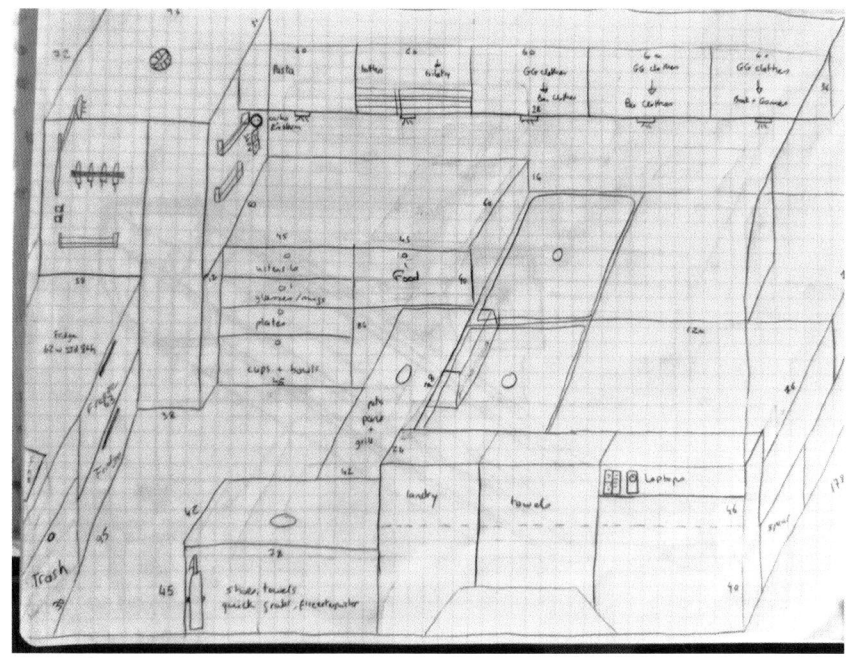

In this layout, the sliding door entrance is at the bottom left corner. On the left of the entrance is the fridge / freezer, and a shower is at the top left corner. Then a small kitchen with drawers and an inverted L-shaped sofa makes up the "living room". The full size bed is elevated in the back. You'll notice a narrow cabinet alongside the bed (bottom right) for laundry, towels and laptop accessories. Up top, a series of 5 hanging cabinets are drawn. Not represented here are the other hanging cabinets on the opposite side.

Obviously, this took many iterations and discussions.

Next, we recommend "taping" the layout to your floor. It helped us a lot by allowing us to actually stand in the space and recognize aspects of our initial design that were unrealistic. We actually changed the size of some cabinets and the shower because of this step.

You'll be able to repeat this step inside the van once you've purchased it, too! You can see here black tape on the floor of the campervan based on our layout. We did make some final updates to the layout based on this step.

Spending time designing the layout of your van is really important. Once your van is built, it isn't like a normal home, where you can move around the furniture -- it's pretty fixed!

We chose for our bed frame to be static, as opposed to having a larger couch area that transforms into a bed at night. We preferred a static bed because we experienced modular layouts in rental campervans before and didn't love to have to transform the layout every night. Also, and more importantly, having a static bed allows us to have a ton of storage underneath, which we really needed. We have so many things in our storage under the bed: two kitesurfs, a kiteboard and harness, a tent, a dozen spearguns, fins, wetsuits, an inflatable boat, a boat motor and battery, extra diesel, yoga mats, and so much more. Much of that space would have been lost with a foldable sofa/bed -- and we prefer to lounge outdoors, anyway.

We also decided to go with a queen bed. Since we have a bit of extra room on one side of the bed, we built a small cabinet alongside the bed. Half of it is used as a "night drawer," with a switch for the lights as well as plugs to charge our phones. We really love this little feature. The other half will be used to house a laundry bag, extra blankets, and other items.

We also decided to have a full indoor shower. To be honest, we didn't agree about this at first. Georgia wasn't convinced we needed it. But after convincing her, building it, and living in the van, we couldn't be happier to have one. And actually, we have two showers. We ended up putting an outdoor shower on the side of the van, because why not? The additional plumbing required for the outdoor shower was super minimal.

Design the Electrical System

Now that you've designed the overall layout of your van, you can proceed to designing the electrical system.

Your campervan electrical system can be pretty basic, almost non-existent. But we'll help you figure out what you need and show you how to design a full electrical system with solar panels, batteries, alternators, and more.

We'll guide through figuring out power sources (and how much power you need), appliances, types of batteries and whether you need one or multiple systems.

Later on in this book, we'll guide you through installing your electrical system. Most of it can be done on your own. The high voltage system (110v or 230v) is typically required to be installed by a professional. While you may prefer hiring a professional to build it all, understanding the different components and how they work together will be important for maintenance and fixes over time.

OVERVIEW:

In a nutshell, a campervan electrical system is quite simple. It includes a battery bank (where energy is stored), charge sources (where energy comes from), and loads (what uses energy).

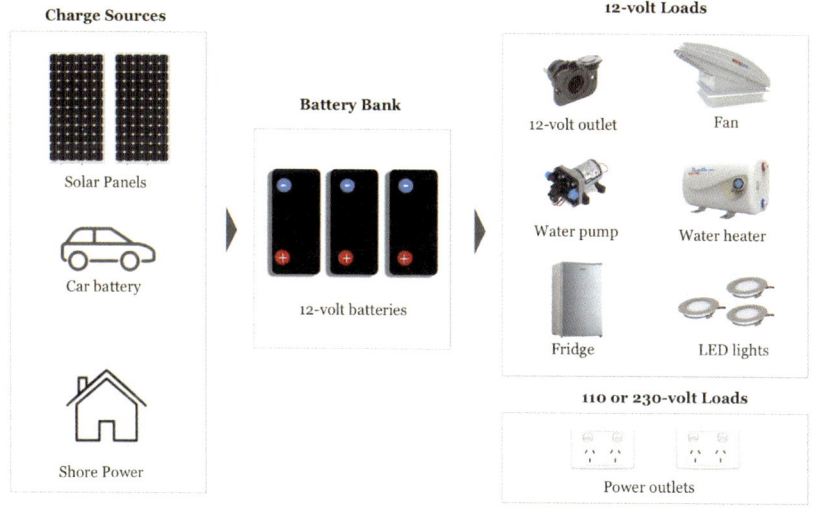

The battery bank is typically composed of multiple 12-volt batteries.

The charge sources can include solar power (solar panels on your roof), an alternator (charging your battery bank while driving), or shore power (charging your battery bank using a plug at a home or campsite).

Loads are what uses energy. In our case, we have a large fridge / freezer, a couple of fans, 14 ceiling lights, an electric shower heater, a pump, and several outlets. Most of these loads are 12-volt DC loads (low voltage). It's also possible to add a high voltage (120 volts in UK, NZ, AU, or 230 volts in Europe and USA) circuit. The high voltage circuit is used to power regular appliances (e.g a blender) or charge laptops and phones.

Note that a high voltage circuit isn't mandatory in a campervan. It adds costs to build one as you'll need a charger / inverter, which are a bit expensive. You'll also need help from a professional to set up high voltage circuits. If you opt out of a high voltage circuit, you will need to have only 12-volt appliances and you won't be able to charge your battery bank using shore power. If cost is an issue, this is definitely a helpful work around.

CHARGE SOURCES:

Solar panels (Item 1 on main electrical diagram):
Most modern campervans have solar panel(s). The number of solar panels you'll need depends on your energy needs. You can estimate how much power you'll need, but it really depends on how long you're planning to be off-grid and whether the sun is shining in your destination. If you're never planning to be off grid more than a day or two, one solar panel and one battery setup should be sufficient. If you'd like to be able to go off-grid for up to a week, then you'll need to consider adding more panels and batteries. While it's possible to try to estimate your exact energy needs, our rule of thumb is that 150W is the minimum, while 500W is plenty.

Most campervans have between 1 and 3 solar panels. Each solar panel typically rates between 100W to 250W. We've opted for 3 solar panels, each 150W.

In order to convert the energy received from the solar panels to charge your battery bank, you'll need to add a solar controller. We opted for a Victron BlueSolar MPPT 100/30, which includes three state charging (more on that later).

Car battery (Item 2 on main electrical diagram):
Charging your battery bank using your car battery while you drive is extremely useful, especially when it's raining, when the solar panels won't help you much. It's fairly easy to set this up. All you need is a Battery Isolator / Alternator. We

recommend purchasing one with a manual override that would allow you to start your car battery using your battery bank in case you accidentally drain your car battery (e.g. by sitting on one beach campsite for too many days). We opted for the Battery Doctor 125 Amp/150 Amp Battery Isolator.

Shore Power (Item 3 on main electrical diagram): If you'd like to be able to charge your battery bank using shore power, you will need a 110V (230V) Charger Converter. This will take your shore power (110V or 230V) and convert it into 12-volt to charge the battery. Since we opted for using shore power and having 110/230V loads, we got a Charger / Inverter combo. The "inverter" function will invert 12-volt current from your battery bank to 120V (or 230V) for regular power outlets. The "charger" function allows you to charge your battery bank using an external power outlet. We opted for a Victron 80/30 MultiPlus Compact, but other cheaper models are likely better value.

BATTERY BANK:

You'll need at least one battery to store the energy and then release it when needed. Most modern campervans have two or three batteries to store more energy.

The amount of energy you need to store depends on how much you'll use. The two things that will likely be using the most energy are your fridge/freezer, as well as your outlets when you're charging things like laptops or phones. If you're using an electric shower heater, it will also use a lot of energy, but only when it's turned on. Lights don't use much.

You can calculate how much energy you'll likely need, but the general rule of thumb is 120 amps is the minimum while 360 amps is a lot.

There are many types of batteries. We recommend getting 12-volt AGM deep cell batteries because of their good value, and it will make things simpler. Alternatively, you can get Lithium batteries which perform and last longer but are much more expensive. We opted for 3 x 120amp 12volt AGM batteries. **(Item 4 on main electrical diagram)**

LOADS:

Except for a couple of high-voltage outlets, all of our loads will be part of our 12-volt DC circuit.

Fridge: There are different types of fridges for campervans, but we recommend using a simple 12-volt fridge.

We spearfish a lot and sometimes catch big fish, so, for us, it was really important to have a lot of freezer space. We opted for a 144L fridge / freezer. We went with the Vitrifrigo DRW180A. Unless you need a decent sized freezer, there are many other great options for cheaper.

Fans: If you're planning on living in your van full-time, or at least for longer than a weekend at a time, then having fans in your van is essential. It will help you keep the van cool when it's hot and avoid smell and fume build up when you cook inside.

Ideally, you'll want to have two fans - one in the front and one in the back - to maximize airflows. You can turn one on to suck air in while the other pushes it out, creating a constant air flow stream.

There are many different types of fans on the market, from low cost options to fancier ones with rain sensors and remote controls. The only must-have is to ensure your fans come with a built-in rain cover.

We opted for 2 Maxx Air fans, because they had good online reviews. We haven't been thrilled, but haven't experienced anything better as of yet.

Ceiling Lights: Make sure to use LED lights to use less power. We opted for some with built in spring clips to make installation easier.

Water Pump: Make sure you read reviews on the pump you select. Select a low noise, high flow pump. We opted for the SHURflo 4009 12V Fresh Water Auto Pump.

Water Heater: We opted for an electric hot water heater. It's 10L and runs on 12 volts. We wish it would heat up more than 10 litres at a time, as it's a bit short for two showers in a row. But given how much power it takes to heat our water, it's probably for the best.

12-volt Outlet Dash Socket: This type of outlet allows you to plug in different 12-volt outlets, USB plugs, or 12-volt appliances. We recommend using the "cigarette lighter" option, then add a removable USB plug, as it's more versatile and won't get outdated as quickly.

Below is a complete diagram of our electrical system. We will break it down and explain how to build it later on in this book.

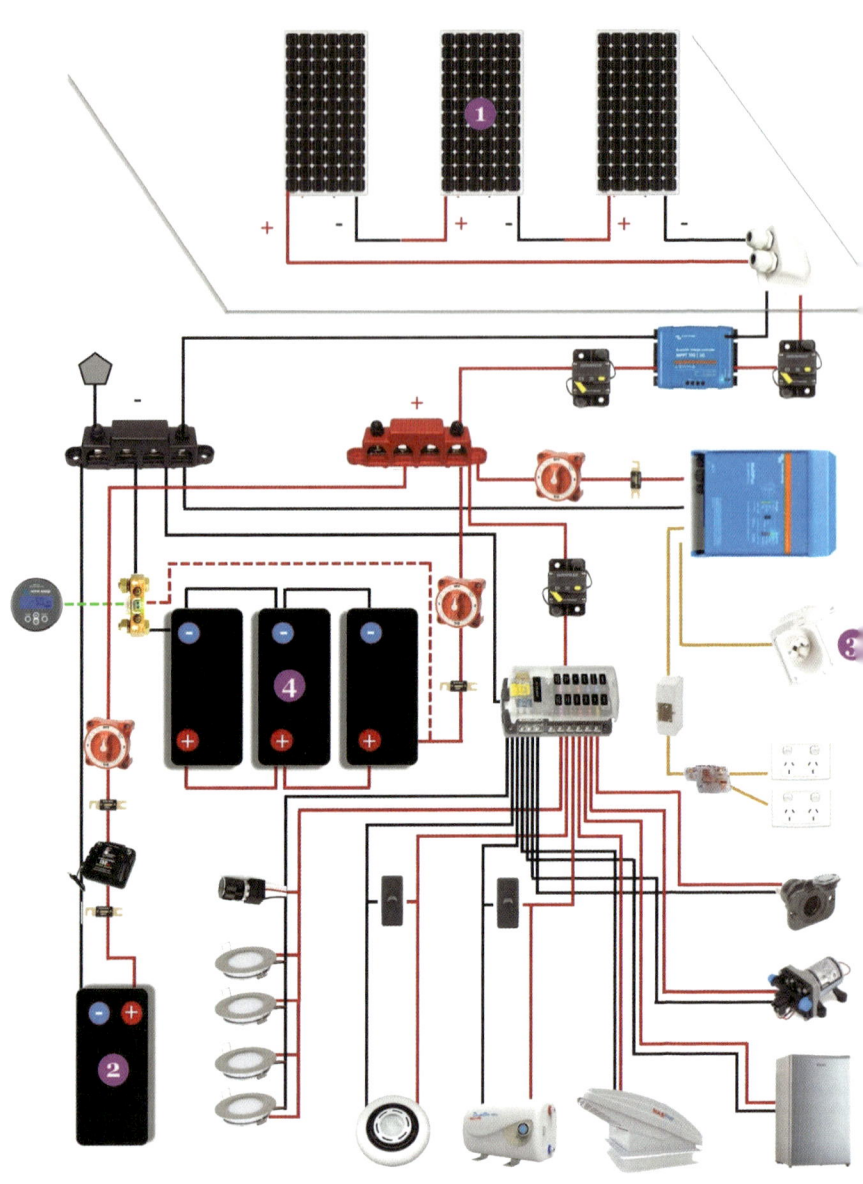

Design the plumbing system

The plumbing system in a campervan is relatively simple (especially after figuring out your electrical system!).

It consists of a fresh water flow (which provides clean water to your shower and sink), and a grey water flow (waste water coming from your sink and shower drains).

The **fresh water flow** has a water inlet (on the van's exterior wall), so you can fill the fresh water tank with water from an external source using a hose. The fresh water tank then holds the fresh water waiting to be used. A pump is used to flow water to the outlets. In our case, our fresh water tank and pump are fixed underneath the van to save space.

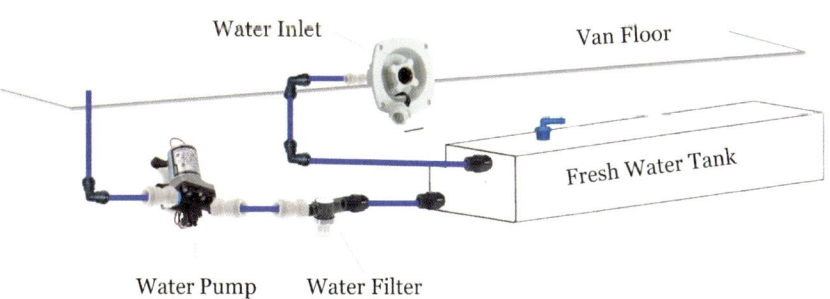

Fresh water tank: We opted for a 110 litre fresh water tank. We managed to find a local company that creates custom water tanks for Sprinter vans.

Water pump: Make sure you read reviews on the pump you select. Select a low noise, high flow pump. We opted for the SHURflo 4009 12V Fresh Water Auto Pump.

Water filter: Note that, unless your pump has a filter included, you must purchase one separately and install it between the fresh water tank and the pump.

Inside the van, we have an indoor **shower and a sink**. We also installed a hot water heater, and plumbing for an outdoor shower.

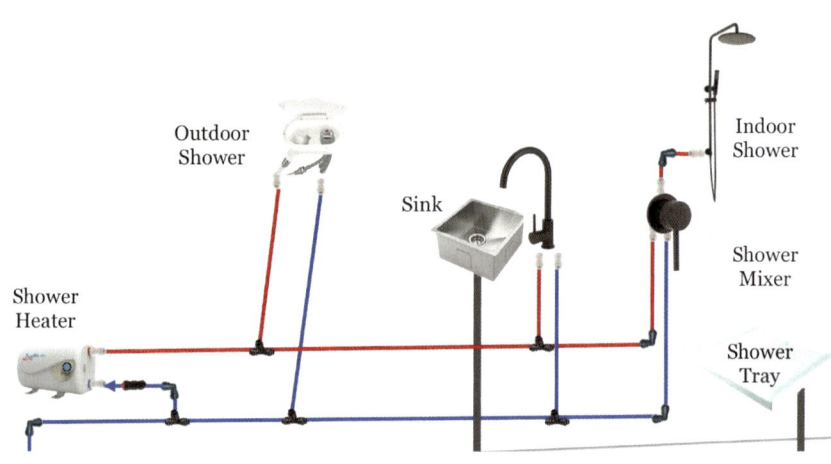

Shower Heater: There are many different types of water heater, including electric or gas powered. We've opted for an electric hot water heater. It can heat 10L at a time, and runs on 12 volts.

The **grey water flows** from the sink and indoor shower drain to a grey water tank. In our case, the grey water tank is fixed underneath the van to save space.

Grey water tank: We opted for a 50 litres grey water tank. You can empty your grey water pretty often, so you don't need to store as much grey water as you do fresh water.

Toilet options: Portable toilets can make living in your caravan more... civilized. We opted for not installing a toilet inside our shower because it would have reduced the space to shower. Instead, we recommend using a dry portable eco-friendly toilet that you can easily store underneath your sink cabinet or sofa. There is a huge range of brands and features. We recommend choosing a toilet that uses eco-friendly additives to prevent unpleasant odours, suppress gas formation and keep the inside of the waste holding tank clean.

Below is a complete diagram of our plumbing system. We will break it down and explain how to build it later on in this book.

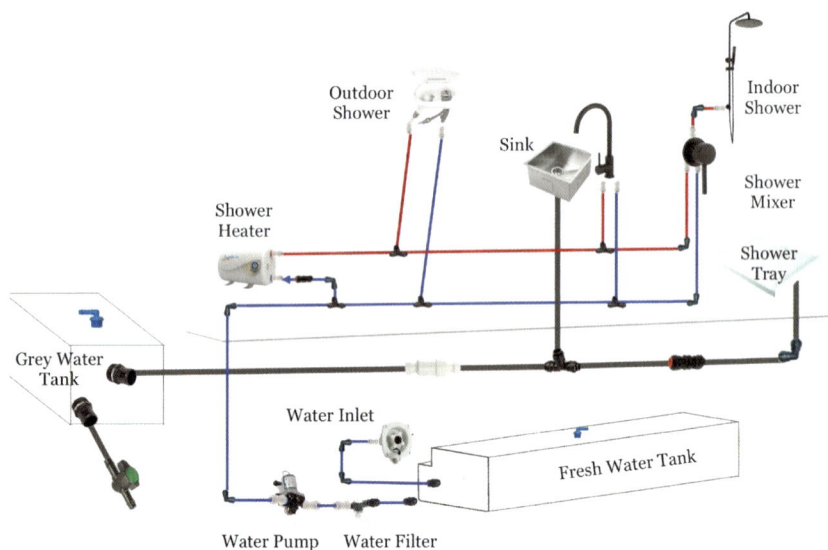

Buy your van

Now it's time to buy your van! How exciting!

Make sure you do your research. There are many sites and marketplaces that list vans or motorhomes. Decide whether you want to buy from a dealership or a private seller. No matter what you decide, make sure to check some critical aspects of the van before you buy it, even if you've decided to buy from a dealer. While there are many honest sellers, some are also ignorant or dishonest.

The manufacturing year and mileage are likely the most important things to check. You may save by buying an older model, but maintenance and repairs costs can add up in the long term. Also make sure to check the maintenance logs to ensure it has been serviced regularly.

When you go check out the van, make sure to take it for a test drive. Open the windows and listen for weird noises. Test the brakes. Look for rust on the inside and outside. Check the air conditioning and heating systems. Does the van have bluetooth or other ways to play music or audiobooks? Finally, check the tires, as they're expensive to replace.

Once you've found a great van, we recommend having it checked by a professional. Inspection costs vary from $50 to $250. Our van only had one previous owner -- a business -- so we opted for a light inspection, just to have peace of mind.

Get the right tools

If, like us, you have no tools, and no friends who have tools, you will need to invest a bit so you can build your van.

Luckily, nowadays there are many cheap options. You can also spend a small fortune -- it depends on whether you plan to keep them after the build, and how comfortable you want your build to be. For us, we only needed them for building our van, and would have to get rid of them afterward, so we opted for the cheapest tools we could find. The only exception is the jigsaw! A cheap jigsaw will likely wobble, not cut straight, and break before you complete your van. Trust us from experience: go with a middle range option for your jigsaw.

Make sure to research the best local hardware store and their return policy. We found that most of them have very easy return policies, so we bought some extra tools just in case and returned what we didn't use at the end.

Here is the list of tools we used for our build:

Item	Picture
Drill Make sure to get a cordless drill. You'll actually really want to have two to avoid having to switch bits and batteries all the time.	
Jigsaw A jigsaw will help you tackle intricate and curved cuts in timber or steel. Given that nothing in a van is straight, this is a must have tool! Make sure you get bits for both wood and metal.	
Mitre Saw A mitre saw will be used to cut most of your structural timber and shiplap. It's extremely easy to use and will save you a lot of time.	
Metal grinder Used to cut metal sheets and plates.	
Holesaw Kit We'd recommend buying a couple of holesaw kits for metal and wood, as you'll need various sizes throughout the build. You can return the ones you haven't used after you're done.	

Stapler
Get either a manual stapler (cheaper) or a stapling gun (more fun). This will only be used for building your sofa cushions.

Caulk Gun
This low cost tool will help you distribute silicone, gap filler, and adhesive cartridges (you'll use a LOT of all of these, but one caulk gun can be repurposed for it all) easily.

Metal file
This will help you remove rough edges on metal parts after cutting them. This is important to cut down on potential rust.

Wire Stripper and Crimper
This will be needed to cut, strip and crimp all your wires. Get a decent one, it will make electrical go much smoother.

Plastic pipe cutter
Used to cut all your water pipes. A clean cut is required to avoid leaks...

Wrench
Used for various purposes during your build.

Utility Knife
A great tool to cut boxes, tape, insulation foam, etc. Consider getting extra blades, as this tool will become your best friend.

39

Leveler
A leveler will help you make sure your structural frames are angled correctly.

Clamps
Use to hold pieces of wood while drying or cutting. You'll probably want ~4-6.

Measuring tape
Pro tip: buy two! You'll always be looking for your measuring tape and they tend to hide all the time. Having a second one will save countless hours. Also, get it in a bright color.

Electrical Tape
This is your new best friend! It is extremely useful in many situations including visualizing floor plans, holding insulation in place temporarily, etc.

Painter's Tape
This will be used to cover surfaces before painting as well as to identify your wires during electrical.

Plumber's Thread Tape
Helps avoid leaks when sealing water pipes. Place the end of the plumber's tape on the thread of the pipe and hold it in place with a finger. Wrap the tape around the pipe in the opposite direction to the direction the pipe will be turned.

Black Marker
This will be used to label your wires, pieces of wood, etc. Get more than you think you'll need, as these also like to hide and are crucial in many steps of the build.

Sandpaper block Used to smooth wood surfaces. We liked using sandpaper blocks better than traditional sandpaper, as they're easier to maneuver.	
Safety Gloves Important to wear when handling insulation wool and sharp metal.	
Safety Mask Important to wear when handling insulation wool or cutting metal parts.	
Safety Goggles Important to wear when handling insulation wool or cutting metal parts.	
Ear Protection (optional) We recommend using these when cutting metal and structural wood.	
Knee Pads (optional) These will protect your knees. We couldn't have built our van without.	
Battery Cable Lug Crimper Hammer (optional) This will allow you to crimp large battery cables. You will need this only if your wire crimper doesn't allow for large (1.5cm+) cables.	

Insulation Aluminium Tape (optional) If you're not able to put insulation between your wires and the outside wall of your van, make sure to tape your wires using this so they do not overheat.	
Right Angle Drill Attachment (optional) We used this drill attachment for difficult to reach drilling.	
Bit Holder Extension Drill Attachment (optional) We used this drill attachment for difficult to reach drilling.	

A few other things to gather, which you likely already own:

- Long pants and long-sleeve shirts: this is CRITICAL for installing your wool insulation, as the tiny glass fibers are super itchy -- for days -- if they get into your skin. Also helpful as you cut wood, metal, etc.
- Hard-toe boots: you will be accidentally dropping heavy things.

Order van-specific supplies

There are many van-specific campervan and motorhome stores. Make sure you do your research. Price can vary greatly.

Once you find a store that you like, if you're planning to buy most of your supplies from it, don't hesitate to reach out to them to ask if they have a trade discount.

We recommend ordering things in advance of your build as it's incredibly frustrating to have to wait for supplies or have to switch the order of your build.

Here are stores that we recommend checking out in various countries (depending on where you're building your van).

AUSTRALIA

caravansplus.	**CaravanPlus** (www.caravansplus.com.au) They have an excellent range of products that are well priced. They ship really fast.
RV Parts EXPRESS	**RV Parts Express** (www.rvpartsexpress.com.au). They have a good range of products and often have lots of products on sale. Fast and cheap shipping.
CAMPSMART	**CampSmart** (www.campsmart.net.au) They have a more limited range of products overall but have great selection in certain categories. Definitely worth checking.
CAMEC making anywhere home	**CAMEC** (www.camec.com.au) They have a more limited range of products online but have good prices on solar panels and appliances.
ARNOLD'S BOAT SHOP	**Arnold's Boat Shop** (www.arnoldsboatshop.com.au) While they aren't a campervan or RV specialist, they have a great selection of plumbing (tanks, water heater, pumps, etc.) and electrical products that you might want to have a look at.

	Atlas Tanks (www.atlastanks.com.au) They offer custom tanks for Mercedes Sprinters and Volkswagen LT vans.
	BCF (www.bcf.com.au) They offer a wide range of caravan and camping accessories. Great to find portable stoves, awnings and more.
	Anaconda (www.anacondastores.com) They have tons of outdoors products for when you're ready to fill your van with awesome toys. Make sure to join their free membership to save.

CANADA

RVPartShop	**RV Part Shop** (www.rvpartshop.ca) They have an excellent range of products that are well priced. They ship fast and free (over $99).
RVSuperstoreCanada.ca	**RV Superstore Canada** (www.rvsuperstorecanada.ca). They have over 10,000 products for your RV build.
RVPartsCanada Your Coast-to-Coast RV Parts Dealer	**RV Parts Canada** (www.rvpartscanada.com) They have an excellent range of products that are well priced. They ship fast and free (over $99).
Marine Outfitters.ca	**Marine Outfitters** (www.marineoutfitters.ca) While they aren't a campervan or RV specialist, they have a great selection of plumbing (tanks, water heater, pumps, etc.) and electrical products that you might want to have a look at.
MEC	**MEC (**www.mec.ca**)** They offer a wide range of outdoors and camping accessories. Great to find portable stoves, awnings and more. Join their membership to save.

SAIL	**Sail (**www.sail.ca**)** They have tons of outdoors products for when you're ready to fill your van with awesome fishing gear.

UNITED KINGDOM

Leisureshop direct	**LeisureShop Direct** (www.leisureshopdirect.com) They have the widest selection we've seen. If you're looking for something, you'll likely find it there.
Homestead Caravans & Outdoor Leisure	**Homestead Caravans** (www.homesteadcaravans.co.uk) They have an excellent range of products that are well priced. They ship fast and free (over £150).
CAMPER INTERIORS	**Camper Interiors** (www.camperinteriors.co.uk) Great if you are renovating an old camper. Easy to get in touch with as well.
FORCE 4 CHANDLERY	**Force4** (www.force4.co.uk) While they aren't a campervan or RV specialist, they have a great selection of plumbing (tanks, water heater, pumps, etc.) and electrical products that you might want to have a look at.
world of CAMPING	**World of Camping** (www.worldofcamping.co.uk) They offer a wide range of outdoors and camping accessories. Great to find portable stoves, awnings and more.

Go Outdoors
(www.gooutdoors.co.uk)
They have tons of outdoors products for when you're ready to fill your van with awesome fishing gear and such.

UNITED STATES

While you can find almost everything on Amazon in the US these days, we find that it is nice to sometimes deal with a smaller store that can give you advice and has a select set of products that are designed to work for your camper build.

RV PARTS COUNTRY — Making the great outdoors even greater	**RV Parts Country** (www.rvpartscountry.com) They have a great selection of products to build your van or motorhome. They have a free hotline you can call with any questions.
iD	**Camper ID** (www.camperID.com) They have over 50,000 products and are well priced. Their website is really well organized and has lots of info on all products.
RV Part Shop	**RV Part Shop** (www.rvpartshop.com) They have a good selection of products and offer free shipping over $99.
BOAT & RV ACCESSORIES	**Boat and RV accessories** (www.boatandrvaccessories.com) They have a great selection of plumbing (tanks, water heater, pumps, etc.), solar and electrical products that you might want to have a look at.

CAMPING WORLD RV & OUTDOORS	**Camping World** (www.campingworld.com) They offer a wide range of rv, outdoors and camping accessories and parts. Plus, they have lots of physical stores so good for those who like to see things before buying.

NEW ZEALAND

℞ WORLD	**RV World** (www.rvworldstore.co.nz) They have a great selection of products. Their selection is designed for modern conversions.
RV Super Centre	**RV Super Centre** (www.rvsupercentre.co.nz) They have an excellent range of products that are well priced. They have good customer support.
Caravan Camping and Marine *Keeping you out there*	**Caravan Camping** (www.caravancamping.co.nz) A smaller shop from Christchurch. They have good selection of product for a modern campervan conversion.
SMART MARINE	**Smart Marine** (www.smartmarine.co.nz) While they aren't a campervan or RV specialist, they have a great selection of fridges, plumbing (tanks, water heater, pumps, etc.) and electrical products that you might want to have a look at.
equipOUTDOORS	**Equip Outdoors** (www.equipoutdoors.co.nz) They offer a wide range of outdoors and camping accessories. Great to find portable stoves, awnings and more.

Select a hardware store

You're going to spend a lot of time at your local hardware store. Make sure to choose one that is close from where you'll be building the van. Despite having done a ton of planning and research, we ended up going back to the store at least a dozen times.

Since you'll be spending a considerable amount of your budget in this store, it's worth comparing prices. Also, make sure to check the return policy. We found that most hardware stores have great return policies and we took advantage of it. We bought a lot more supplies that we needed and ended up returning a lot of it. It saved us several trips! It's not fun having to stop a task because you're out of screws.

Plumbing: Know-How

TIPS & TRICKS

Before you get started with plumbing, you need to know how to correctly connect pipes to one another, and to fittings.

For the entire fresh water flow we used 12mm pipes with John Guest push-on fittings. It made it really easy to connect pipes.

Cold water pipes:
You'll use 12mm blue pipes for cold water. Use a plastic pie cutter for a clean and straight cut. Put the pipe into the John Guest push-on fitting. Push hard until you hear a click, then a second. Slightly pull the pipe outwards and place a red locking clip to secure the pipe.

Hot water pipes:
Repeat the same process for the hot water pipes. Simply insert a hot water insert into the pipe prior to pushing it into the fitting.

Grey water pipes:
You'll use 25mm flexible PVC tubes for the grey water pipes. Use PVC glue to glue the pipe to the fitting. Insert a hose clamp and tighten it near the end of the pipe.

Electrical Wiring: Know-How

TIPS & TRICKS

Before you build your electrical system, you'll need to know how to properly connect wires together.

There are several ways to connect wires, but our preferred method is crimping, since it provides a superior hold and is easy.

Step 1: Use a wire striper to strip about 1 cm of plastic covering from the wire. Repeat the same process on the second wire.

Step 2: Use an insulated double crimp connector. Insert a stripped wire on one end. Crimp the wire in place using a crimper. Just press really hard. Try pulling the wire to ensure the wire is secured. Repeat for the second wire on the other end.

Step 3: Tape the entire connector and joints using electrical tape.

Alternatively, if you want a cleaner looking wrap, you can use heat shrink tubing. Simply insert a small piece of tubing prior to crimping the wires. Once both wires are crimped, place the tubing in the center and shrink it using a hair dryer. We didn't do this, as all of our wires are hidden and the tape method is easier.

Cutting Weird Shapes: Know-How

TIPS & TRICKS

One of the hardest parts of building a campervan is that there are no straight edges. Everything is shaped pretty weird.

In order to properly cut plywood to the right shapes to mirror the shape of the campervan, we used a cardboard wheel to trace the shape onto the plywood.

Step 1: Trace a circle on a piece of cardboard. You can use a paint can or anything else you have that is circular. Cut the circle using scissors. Drill a small hole in the middle and push a black marker through.

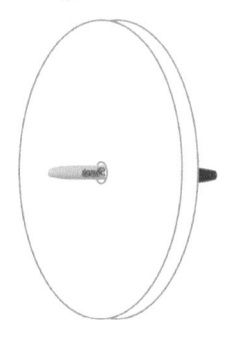

Step 2: Say you need to cut a piece of plywood to fit the top corner of your van where the car walls meet the ceiling. Place the plywood as closely as possible to the corner. Use your disk to trace the shape of the wall onto the plywood by simply wheeling the disk following the wall. That's it! You'll now have the exact shape traced and you can use a jigsaw to cut the plywood to shape.

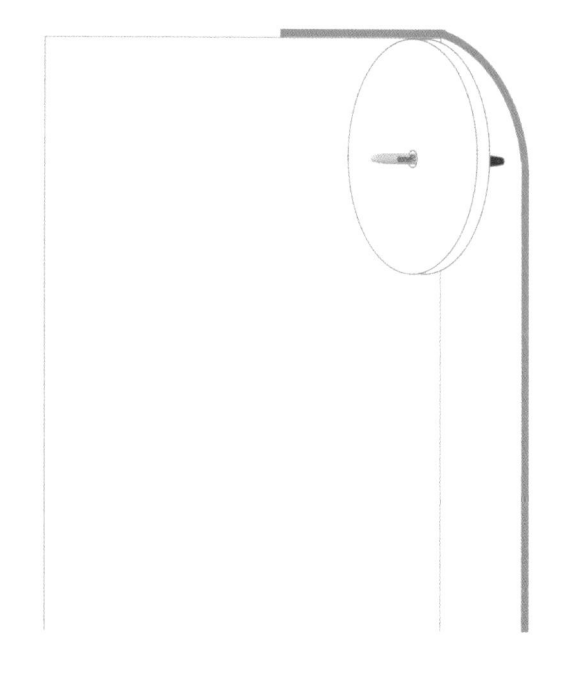

Part 4: Build Your Van in 21 Days

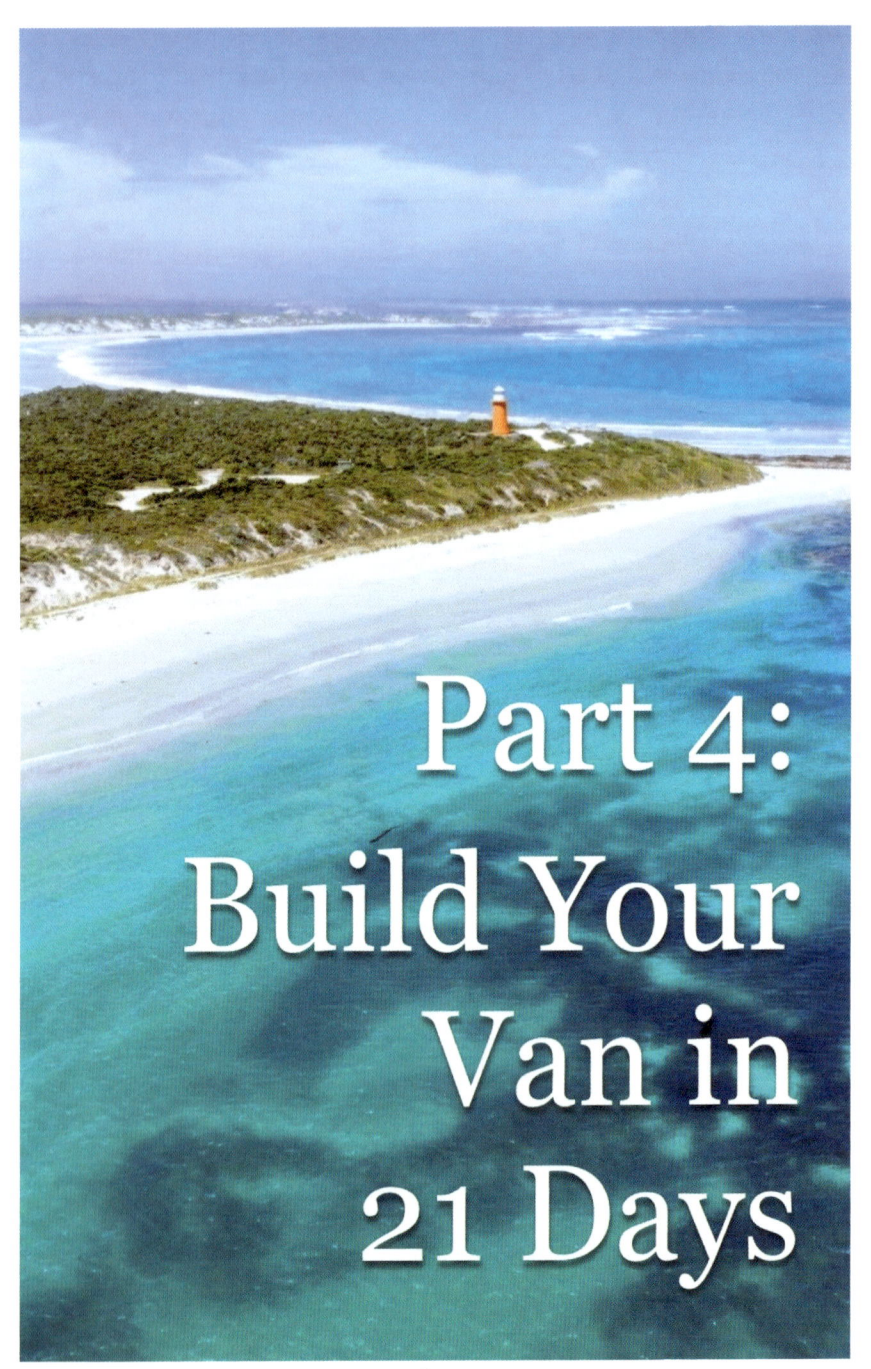

In this section, we will detail how to build your campervan in just 21 days! While this might seem optimistic, it's actually totally doable. We did it! We built our first campervan ever, with zero experience, in just 3 weeks. In order to achieve this timeframe, you need to have carefully planned the layout and design of your van.

You may decide not to follow the exact order, but the following steps are what we think makes the most sense to optimize your build and make it as easy and speedy as possible.

Day 1: Fans installation

If you're planning on living in your van full-time, or at least for longer than a weekend at a time, then having fans in your van is essential. It will help you keep the van cool when it's hot and avoid smell and fume build up when you cook.

Ideally, you'll want to have two fans - one in the front and one in the back - to maximize airflows. You can turn one on to suck air in while the other pushes it out.

There are many different types of fans on the market, from low cost options to fancier ones with rain sensors and remote controls. The only must-have is to ensure your fans come with a built-in rain cover.

Before you install your fan(s) -- which means cutting a huge hole in your roof -- make you sure you have properly planned your roof layout. You want to make sure you have enough room for your solar panels (likely 2 or 3), your fan(s), and possibly your shower air vent if you're planning to add a shower. In our set up, we've opted for 3 x 150W solar panels, 2 Maxx Air fans, and an air vent for our shower's fan. It all fits perfectly on our long-wheelbase Mercedes Sprinter van.

SUPPLIES NEEDED

Item	Qty	Picture
12-Volt Fan We recommend the Maxx Air fans. They come with a rain cover and remote. They're low profile and quiet.	2	
Sikaflex Pro This is a polyurethane elastic sealant, great for interior and exterior joints with excellent water, weather and ageing resistance. Make sure you buy it in whatever color your van is, or use clear.	2	
Weather Seal Tape Self-adhesive surface mounted weather seal for windows and doors.	1	
Rust Protector Paint This paint will prevent rust from forming on the roof of your van after you cut your hole(s).	1	
Paint Brush	1	

TOOLS NEEDED

Item	Picture
Drill Make sure to get a cordless drill. You'll actually really want to have two to avoid having to switch bits and batteries all the time.	
Jigsaw A jigsaw will help you tackle intricate and curved cuts in timber or steel. Given that nothing in a van is straight, this is a must have tool! Be sure you get bits for metal for this project.	
Electrical Tape Any color will work, as you'll be removing / hiding the tape at the end.	
Caulk Gun This will help you distribute your silicone gap filler easily.	
Metal file This will help you remove rough edges after you cut holes in your van, and help prevent the holes from rusting.	

STEP-BY-STEP GUIDE

We realize that this step might be a bit overwhelming! You probably just bought your van and the very first step is to cut a giant hole in the roof. However, installing the fans is actually pretty easy and we'll guide you through it all.

Step 1: Use electrical tape to outline a square the required size, with the inside of the tape indicating the correct measurements. The installation guide of your fan will indicate the exact measurements. We liked using tape better than a marker because you can double check your measurement and still adjust the tape as needed. The tape also makes the jigsaw cut smoother.

Step 2: Drill a hole in one of the corners using a drill bit wide enough for your jigsaw's blade to fit in. Make sure you drill the hole so that the <u>outside</u> of the hole touches the inside of the tape. Repeat at each corner.

Step 3: Use the jigsaw to cut the square hole. Make sure to go slow and apply downward pressure on the jigsaw.

Step 4: Use a metal file to smooth the edge of your cut. Clean the surface, then apply some rust protector paint. Let it dry.

Step 5: Cut your weather seal tape to cover the edges of your cut. If the roof of your van has grooves, you can use multiple layers of tape to create a flat surface.

Step 6: Place the top cover of your fan on the tape and use the provided screws to secure it in place. Use Sikaflex on the top (outside) and bottom (inside) as well as on the top of each screw cap. You don't want rain to get in! Carefully slide the fan in the hole and fix it using the provided screws.

Step 7 (optional): You may need to add small pieces of timber on the inside of the roof to ensure the screws are properly secured.

Step 8: Make sure to remove all metal debris from your roof, otherwise they will likely create rust.

That's it! You've completed your first major step in building your van. If you'd like to test your fans right away, you can connect them to a 12-volt battery. Otherwise, you'll have to wait a few more days until we tackle the electrical systems.

Day 2: Solar Panels

Now that you've installed your fans, you must be comfortable being on the roof of your van! So, let's keep working on the roof today, and install our solar panels.

Most campervans have between 1 and 3 solar panels. Each solar panel typically rates between 100W to 250W. You can estimate how much power you'll need (more on this in the planning section of this book), but it really depends on how long you're planning to be off-grid and whether the sun is likely to be shining at your destination. If you're never planning to be offgrid more than a day or two, one solar panel and one battery setup should be sufficient. If you'd like to be able to go off-grid for up to a week, then you'll need to consider adding more panels and batteries. We've opted for 3 solar panels, each 150W.

SUPPLIES NEEDED

Item	Qty	Picture
Solar Panels We recommend using "sturdy" solar panels because they're more reliable and efficient. However, if you have a pop-up roof, you may want to use "flexible" solar panels as they are lighter. We've opted for sturdy 150W Mono-Cristalline panels.	3	
Solar Cable - 6mm2 This cable is ideal for connecting your outdoor solar panels to your solar regulator. It's UV protected.	20m	
Sikaflex Pro This is a polyurethane elastic sealant, great for interior and exterior joints with excellent water, weather and ageing resistance. Make sure you buy it in whatever color your van is or use clear.	2	
Solar Panel brackets (optional) If your roof has grooves, you may want to purchase brackets. It also makes it easier to remove the panels when needed.	3	
Solar Connector MC4 (optional) These waterproof connectors make it easy to disconnect your solar system to change or fix it. If you don't want to use these, you can simply use regular cable joiners.	4	

Double Cable Entry Point (optional) A cable entry point is used where your cables enter your van roof. It allows you to give a neat waterproof entry. Alternatively, you can just drill holes and use Sikaflex to waterproof the entry point.	1	

TOOLS NEEDED

Item	Picture
Drill Make sure to get a cordless drill. You'll actually really want to have two to avoid having to switch bits and batteries all the time.	
Caulk Gun This low cost tool will help you distribute silicone, gap filler & adhesive cartridges easily. You can repurpose from your fan installation.	
Wire Stripper and Crimper This will be needed to cut, strip, and crimp all your wires. Don't get the cheapest one here -- this tool will make your life a lot easier!	

STEP-BY-STEP GUIDE

Fixing your solar panels on your roof is pretty easy. Make sure you get someone to help, because the panels are pretty heavy and thus hard to get up onto your roof alone.

Wiring the solar panels is also pretty easy. Below is a diagram to help you figure out how to wire your solar panels in series. There is a large debate all over the internet as to whether you should wire your panels in series or in parallel. The main difference between series and parallel circuits is that, in series circuits, all components are connected in series so that they all share the same current; whereas, in parallel circuits, components are connected in parallel so that they all have the same potential difference between them. It's a long story and a wild debate, but let's cut things short! For 99% of campervan set-ups, it's best to wire panels in series. It's easier, requires less equipment, and works better in most sun conditions.

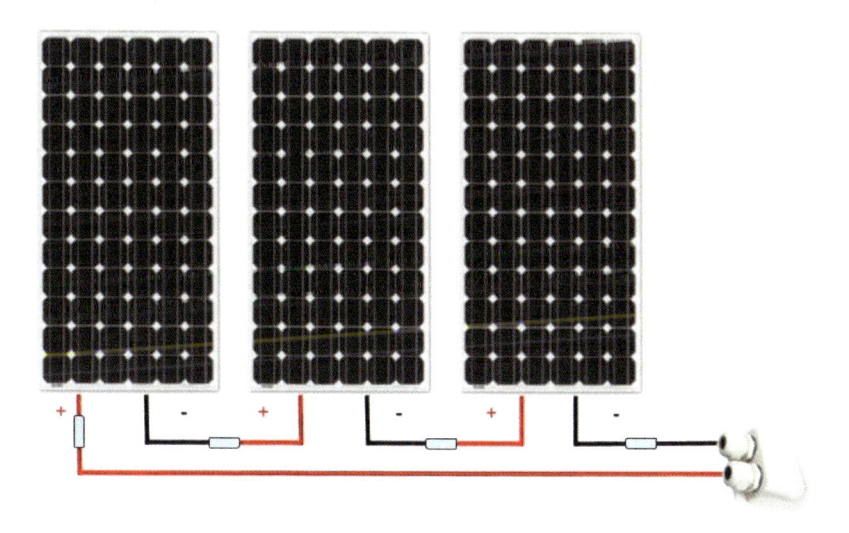

Step 1: Get the solar panel(s) on the roof and make sure the layout works well. If you're using solar panel brackets, fix them on the roof using the provided screws. Make sure to use Sikaflex to ensure it's sealed and waterproof.

Step 2: Start wiring the solar panels in series (using the diagram above). Use the MC4 connectors or a cable joiner to connect the cables.

Step 3: Fix the solar panels onto the solar panel brackets and drill two holes for the wires to enter the van. Optionaly, fix the double cable entry point onto the roof using Sikaflex

Step 4: Once again, make sure to remove all metal debris from your roof, otherwise it will likely create rust.

That's it! If you have a volt meter, you can now test your solar panels. If not, you'll have to wait a couple of days until the electrical system is in place.

Day 3: Electrical roughing

Today, we'll be tackling the electrical roughing. This consists of laying out all wires that you will need for your van. It's important to do this step early in the build because it's obviously way easier to fit in cables before you put in the insulation and walls.

For this part to be successful, you will need to have carefully planned the layout of the van, including where all the plugs and all the lights will go. You will also need to decide where your main electrical system and monitors will go. So, if you haven't done this yet, go back to the planning section.

Also of note, it is better to have extra cable than not enough -- especially given you'll be running it behind cabinets, above ceiling finishes, etc. Rule of thumb here is to leave an extra foot or so than you think you need for each cable segment.

SUPPLIES NEEDED

Item	Qty	Picture
Solar Cable - 6mm2 This cable is ideal for connecting your outdoor solar panels to your solar regulator. They're UV protected	20m	
2 Gauge Battery Cable This cable is ideal for connecting batteries together.	10m	
Twin Cable - 4mm, 15 amp This low amperage cable is ideal for connecting all your 12-volt systems (lights, fans, fridge, etc.).	60m	
Twin & Earth Cable - 2.5 mm This cable will be used for connecting your high voltage (i.e. regular) plugs.	20m	
Sikaflex Pro This is a polyurethane elastic sealant, great for interior and exterior joints with excellent water, weather and ageing resistance. Make sure you buy it in whatever color your van is or use clear.	1	

TOOLS NEEDED

Item	Picture
Drill Make sure to get a cordless drill. You'll actually really want to have two to avoid having to switch bits and batteries all the time.	
Electrical Tape Any color will do, as this is to help mark and hold up your cables until you build structural items around them.	
Painter's Tape This will be used to label / identify your wires.	
Insulation Aluminium Tape (optional) If you're not able to put insulation between your wires and the outside wall of your van, make sure to tape your wires using this to protect them from heat.	
Wire Stripper and Crimper This will be needed to cut, strip, and crimp all your wires.	
Black Marker This will be used to label your wires.	

STEP-BY-STEP GUIDE

Laying out the cables is quite easy. Start where your main electrical system (i.e your batteries, fuse boxes, controllers, etc.) will live, then insert the cables through the van's walls and roof as needed. Try avoiding putting cables below your floor (as the weight of your bed, gear and furniture can crush them) and instead go around via the walls and ceiling.

Step 1: Determine where your main electrical system will be. In our case, we've decided to build it on top of the driver-side back wheel. Make sure that you'll be able to easily access your electrical system in case you need to switch a fuse or repair something.

Step 2: Lay out the cables starting at your electrical system base to each "end point" -- for example your lights, or fans. See next section for detailed pictures of our layout.

Step 3: Make sure to leave extra wire's length at each end, and use painter's tape to label each wire (e.g "front fan" or "kitchen lights").

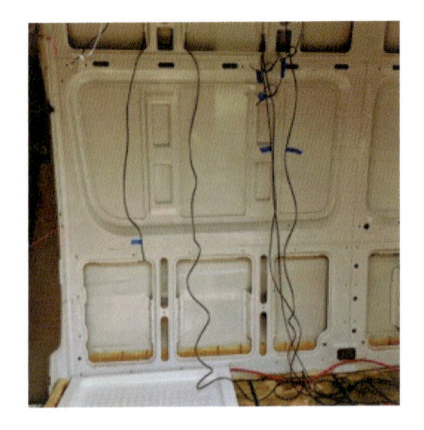

Step 4: Use the existing holes in the sides or roof of the van or drill additional holes / tape up as needed. Use Sikaflex to "glue" wires to avoid them rubbing through holes and getting damaged with vibrations when you're driving. Use electrical tape to neatly wrap wires together.

Step 5: In places where you may not be able to put insulation between the wires and the sides of the van, wrap insulation tape around your wires to avoid them melting on hot days.

In the next section, we will outline our cable layout. Each cable goes from our "electrical system base" next to the driver-side back wheel. We colour coded the wires for ease of description only.

Note: this is of course the layout for our van, so you will need to adjust all of the outputs to reflect your van layout.

FRONT CABLES LAYOUT:

Red cable: This cable goes from the "electrical system base" to where our fridge will be. Use Twin Cable - 4mm, 15 amp for this. If you have a large fridge / freezer, you may want to use slightly thicker wire to avoid voltage drops. We used a 8mm twin cable.

Purple cable: This cable goes from the "electrical system base" to the car battery. This will be used to connect the alternator / isolator to charge your batteries while driving. Use 2 Gauge Battery Cable for this.

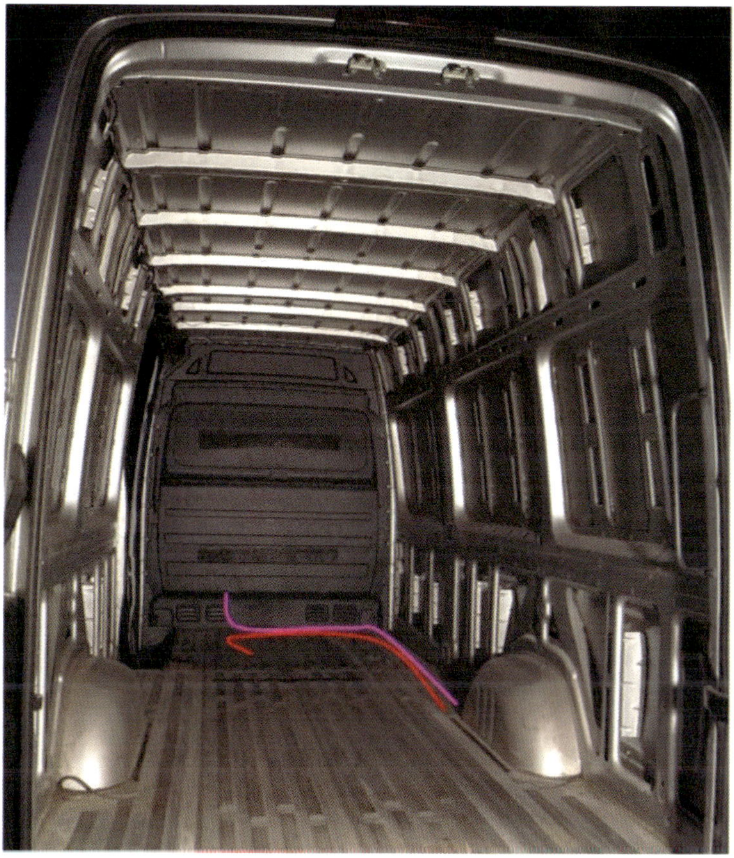

SOLAR CABLES LAYOUT:

Orange cables: These cables go from the "electrical system base" to the entry point of your solar system. Use **two** Solar Cables - 6mm2 for this (one each for negative and positive connections).

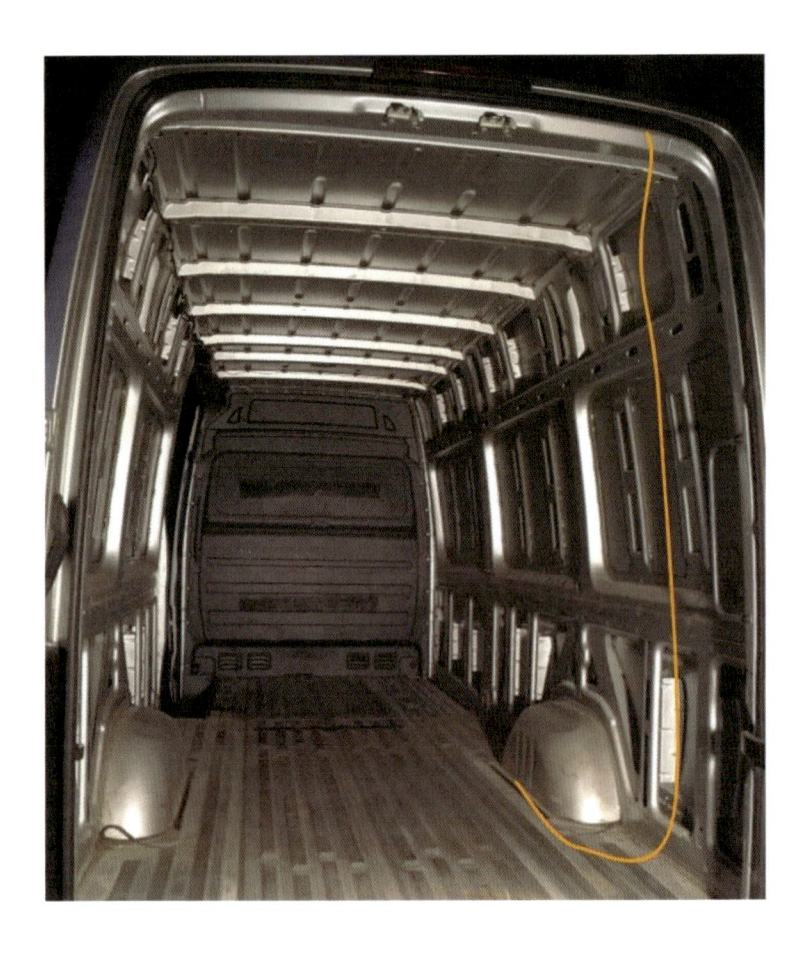

FAN CABLES LAYOUT:

Green cable: This cable goes from the "electrical system base" to the front fan. Use Twin Cable - 4mm, 15 amp.

Turquoise cable: This cable goes from the "electrical system base" to the back fan. Use Twin Cable - 4mm, 15 amp.

Note: We didn't need any switches for our fans since they come with a remote and manual on/off switch on them.

LIGHT CABLES LAY OUT:

Green cable: This cable goes from the "electrical system base" to the front light of the 5 roof lights set. Note that this cable goes through the shower wall, where a switch will be added (green square) to turn the lights on and off. You can label the switch using painter's tape for now (you'll cut it and install the switch or dimmer later on). Use Twin Cable - 4mm, 15 amp for this.

Turquoise cable: This cable goes from the "electrical system base" to the 4 lights underneath the driver-side hanging cabinets. Note that this cable goes through the shower wall where a switch will be added (turquoise square). You can label the switch using painter's tape for now (you'll cut it and install the switch or dimmer later on). Use Twin Cable - 4mm, 15 amp for this.

Red cable: This cable goes from the "electrical system base" to the 5 lights underneath the passenger-side hanging cabinets. Note that this cable goes to the "bed-side drawer" where a switch will be added (red square). You can label the switch using painter's tape for now (you'll cut it and install the switch or dimmer later on). Use Twin Cable - 4mm, 15 amp for this.

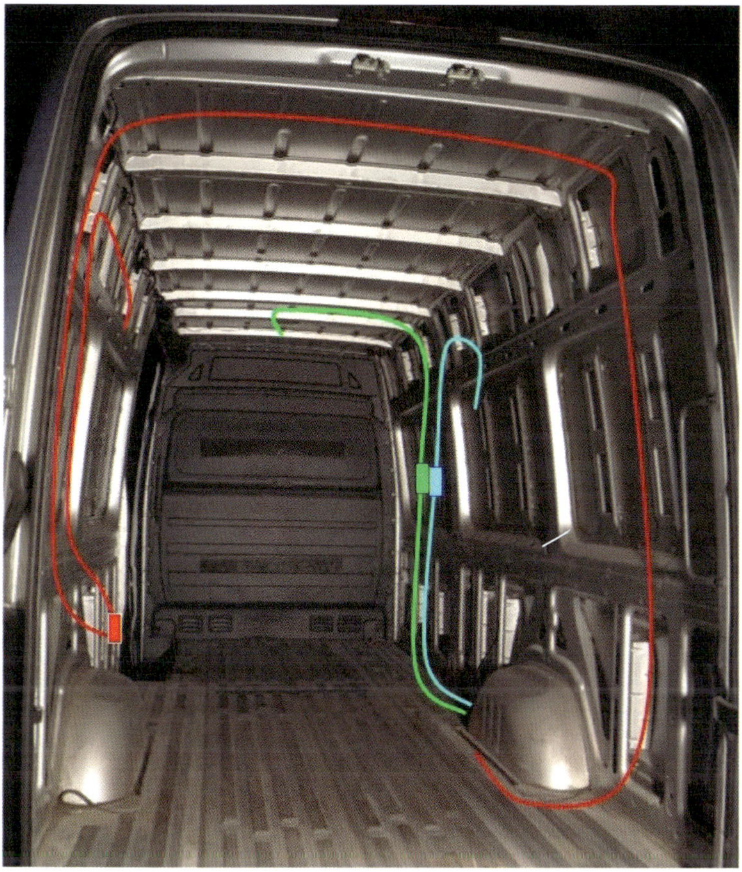

PLUG CABLES LAY OUT:

Blue cables: These cables go from the "electrical system base" to the "kitchen electrical panel" that is located on the shower wall. Use Twin Cable - 4mm, 15 amp for 12-volt cigarette lighter plugs and use Twin & Earth Cable - 2.5 mm for higher-voltage plugs.

Purple cables: Repeat the step above for the plugs in the back of the van. In our case, we decided to add a cigarette lighter plug and higher-voltage plug in our "bed-side drawer."

PUMP AND WATER HEATER CABLES LAY OUT:

Red cable: This cable goes from the "electrical system base" to the pump underneath the van. Use Twin Cable - 4mm, 15 amp for this.

Blue cable: This cable goes from the "electrical system base" to the "kitchen electrical panel," where a switch will be added then back to the "electrical system base," where the water heater will be located. Use Twin Cable - 4mm, 15 amp for this.

SHOWER LIGHT & FAN CABLE LAY OUT:

Orange cable: This cable goes from the "electrical system base" to the shower light & fan. Note that this cable goes through the shower wall where a switch will be added (orange square). You can label the switch using painter's tape for now (you'll cut it and install the switch or dimmer later on). Use Twin Cable - 4mm, 15 amp for this.

Day 4: Walls Insulation

Insulation is important to maintain a comfortable van temperature when it's cold or hot outside. It also helps reduce noise. There are many different ways (and opinions on how) to insulate your van - from foam boards, to spray foam, to fiberglass, to reflective foil.

We opted for insulation glasswool, a.k.a earth wool. It's typically made from recycled glass and sand. It works great for vans because it's extremely easy to use in the many weird crevasses. It's also a great thermal insulator and helps reduce noises from outside. And best of all, it's made from recycled materials!

Note: Make sure to wear safety goggles, mask, and gloves, as well as a long-sleeve shirt and pants to avoid getting in contact with small glass particles. These are EXTREMELY uncomfortable and will stay in your skin for days despite showers. Trust us.

SUPPLIES NEEDED

Item	Qty	Picture
Insulation Glasswool We opted for this insulation made of recycled glass and sand because it improves acoustic and thermal performance and is extremely easy to install in a van	40m²	
Sikaflex Pro You can purchase any color, as this will be used to hold the wool to the van walls and ceiling.	2	

TOOLS NEEDED

Item	Picture
Utility Knife You'll use this to cut insulation into appropriate sizes.	
Painter's Tape This will be used to help hold the insulation up to the wall and ceiling.	
Caulk Gun You can repurpose this from your previous days' work.	
Safety Gloves VERY important to wear when handling insulation wool.	
Safety Mask VERY important to wear when handling insulation wool.	
Safety Goggles VERY important to wear when handling insulation wool.	

STEP-BY-STEP GUIDE

Step 1: Lay down the glass wool and start cutting it into appropriate sized pieces, using a utility knife.

Step 2: Fill in all cavities with glass wool. For larger holes, use Sikaflex to glue the pieces to the walls.

Step 3: Make sure the electric cables are on the "inside" of the van -- not between the wall and the insulation -- to avoid them melting when it gets hot.

Step 4: You can use tape to ensure larger pieces don't fall down. Don't worry about it holding for a long period of time, since you'll be adding plywood / timber to your walls soon.

That's it! Your wall insulation is done. Pretty easy, heh!? You can now add thin plywood to your walls if you've opted for this solution as a wall covering. Later on, we'll cover the visible part of the walls using shiplap.

Day 5: Shower Framing

If you've decided to build an indoor shower, then building the frame of it is the first step toward adding this (luxurious!) part of your build.

Building the shower isn't the easiest part of the van build, as it's likely fitting into an uneven "rectangle" of the van -- and because it obviously needs to be waterproof. But it is worth it: after a long hike or day at the beach, it is SO nice to enjoy a hot shower!

SUPPLIES NEEDED

Item	Qty	Picture
Shower Tray We opted for a 83cm x 67cm tray designed for a campervan. It's large enough to shower. If you plan to also have a fixed toilet in the shower, then select one a bit wider.	1	
Structural Pine Timber: 35x75mmx2.4m This pine is ideal for framing your shower, bed and sofa.	10	
2440x1220x6mm AA Grade Marine Plywood This plywood is ideal for your shower walls.	3	
Batten screws Use 45mm to 65mm batten screws to screw structural wood together.	100	
Timber screws Use 25mm to 45mm timber screws to screw plywood together.	100	
Angle Brackets Use a variety of angle brackets to support your timber frames.	20	

TOOLS NEEDED

Item	Picture
Drill Make sure to get a cordless drill. You'll actually really want to have two to avoid having to switch bits all the time.	
Jigsaw A jigsaw will help you tackle the intricate and curved cuts in the timber for your shower.	
Mitre Saw A mitre saw will be used to cut your structural timber for your shower. It's extremely easy to use and will save you a lot of time.	
Leveler A leveler will help you make sure your shower frames are angled correctly.	
Clamps Use to hold pieces of wood while drying.	
Measuring tape Pro tip: buy two! You'll always be looking for your measuring tape and they tend to hide all the time. Having a second one will save countless hours.	

STEP-BY-STEP GUIDE

Step 1: Lay down the shower tray. Locate the drain hole(s) on the tray. In our case, our tray had two options for the drain hole. Figure out a position that will ensure you can drill a hole through the floor of the van for the drain without messing with the van's function. Secure the tray with structural pine timber and batten screws. Notice that for the right side of the shower we used the wide side of the wood. This is to allow for enough space in the "back wall" of our shower to accommodate electrical wires and water pipes. Do not fix the shower tray to the floor of the van yet -- just use it as a placeholder to do your framing.

Step 2: Build up the sides of the shower using structural pine timber. Use your leveler to ensure the walls are straight. The "back wall" (the right edge of the shower in the previous photo), shown here, will be used to house the water pipes (as well as electrical wires for the fans, lights, and plugs).

Step 3: Use marine plywood to build the inside walls and roof of the shower. Notice the fridge and car battery cables on the floor. These will go underneath the shower tray to the front of the van.

Step 4: Put back the shower tray and ensure you have enough room to shower!

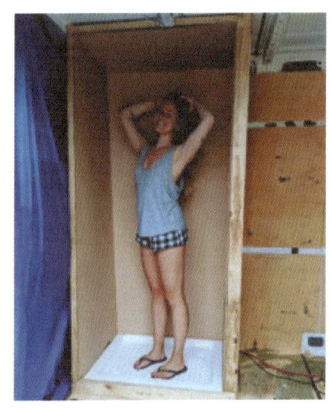

Step 5: Build in the front frame ensuring you have enough room to get in and out of the shower. Use your leveler to ensure the walls are straight.

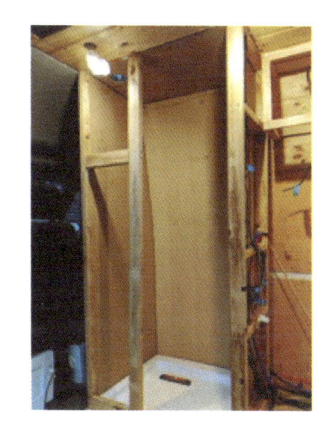

Step 6: Use marine plywood to build the last inside wall

That's it for now! The first (and easiest) part of building the shower is done.

Day 6: Fresh Water Tank

Now that you have framed your shower, you need to ensure you can secure the fresh water tank. Since we've opted for placing the fresh water tank underneath the van (and under the shower), fixing the tank before finishing building the rest of the shower is important.

The fresh water tank, when full, will be heavy! Ours is 110 litres - when full, that's 110kg. The last thing you want is for your water tanks to fall off when you hit a road bump, so you need to make sure they're fully secured.

We used a simple system to hold our tanks in place: in the front and back of the tank, we fixed two metal rods on each side joined by a metal plate. Simple but very secure.

SUPPLIES NEEDED

Item	Qty	Picture
Fresh Water Tank This tank will contain your fresh water - the water used for your shower and tap. The bigger, the better, as you always use more water than you think.	1	
M10 Threaded Stainless Steel Rod These metal rods will be used to fix your water tanks underneath the van. You can use a metal grinder to cut them to size.	4	
M10 Stainless Steel Washer These washers will be placed before the nut to ensure the rod is secured in place.	8	
M10 Stainless Steel Lock Nut Make sure to buy the "Lock Nut" type to make sure the rod stays secured even when the van vibrates as you're driving.	8	
Aluminium Flat Bar Make sure it's at least 3 mm x 10mm so it can sustain the weight of your tank when full.	1	

Water Tank Sender Arm (optional) A tank sender probe is installed into the side of the water tank, then simply connected to the gauge inside the van to monitor the water level in your tanks.	1	
12 mm Pipe - Clear We used this pipe for the water "overflow" or "breather" pipe but you can use 12mm John Guest Pipe if you'd like.	1m	
Screw In Outlet Breather Make sure you get the right size to fit your tank hole and breather pipe.	1	
Mesh Screen (optional) You can tape a little piece of mesh screen at the tip of your overflow pipe to avoid insects getting into your tanks.	1m	
Pipe Retaining Clips These will be used to clip the pipes to the car fuselage.	2	
PVC Pipe Glue Used to secure pipes to their connectors.	1	

TOOLS NEEDED

Item	Picture
Drill Make sure to get a cordless drill. You'll actually really want to have two to avoid having to switch bits all the time.	
Holesaw Kit We'd recommend buying a couple of holesaw kits for metal and wood as you'll need various sizes throughout the build. You can return the ones you haven't used after you're done!	
Plastic Pipe Cutter Used to cut all your water pipes. A clean cut is required to avoid leaks	
Metal Grinder Used to cut metal sheets and plates.	
Plumber's Thread Tape Helps avoid leaks when sealing water pipes. Place the end of the plumber's tape on the thread of the pipe and hold it in place with a finger. Wrap the tape around the pipe in the opposite direction to the direction the pipe will be turned.	
Wrench Used for various purposes during your build.	

STEP-BY-STEP GUIDE

Step 1: Drill a hole using the appropriate holesaw (refer to your chosen water tank sender arm manual) towards the top of your tank. Make sure the bottom of the arm reaches the bottom of the tank. Clean your tank with a hose to rid of debris.

Step 2: Insert the water tank sender arm and tighten it using a wrench. Using plumber's tape, screw in the outlet breather to the tank's breather hole (typically the hole at the top of the tank). Secure the "breather pipe" to the outlet breather. Use PVC glue to secure the pipe.

Step 3: Once the breather pipe (clear pipe on the picture) and the sender arm are secured, you are ready to fix the water tank underneath the van.

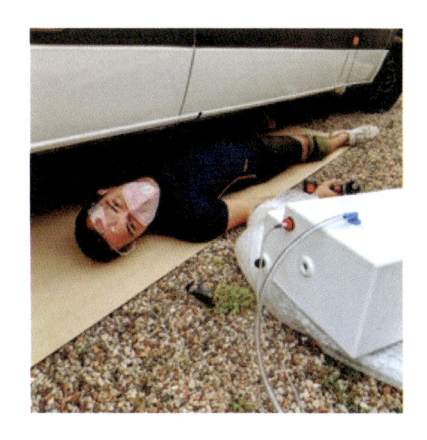

Step 4: Carefully secure the tank using M10 rod, washers, nuts and metal bar. See diagram below. Once done, you can secure the breather pipe to the car fuselage using retaining clips. The breather pipe will "leak" water out of your tank when it's full. Make sure the end of the breather pipe is unobstructed. Optionally, you can tape a small piece of mesh screen at the end of the breather pipe to prevent insects from crawling into your tank.

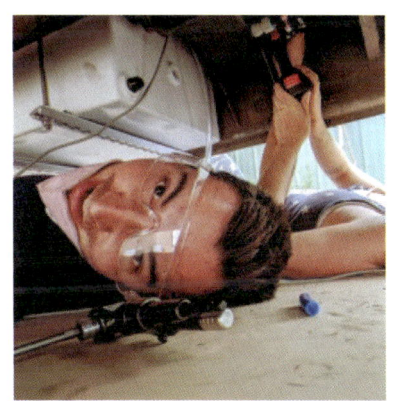

More in depth: To secure your water tank underneath the van, drill 10mm holes through the metal plate on each side of the front of your water tank. Insert the M10 threaded rods. Using a metal grinder, carefully cut your metal plate to the right size (if needed). Drill holes up through the floor of the van to accommodate the metal rods. Secure the rods using washers and nuts on both ends. Use your metal grinder to cut off excess length inside the van.

Repeat for the back of the water tank.

If your water tank is long, you may add a third plate in the middle as well.

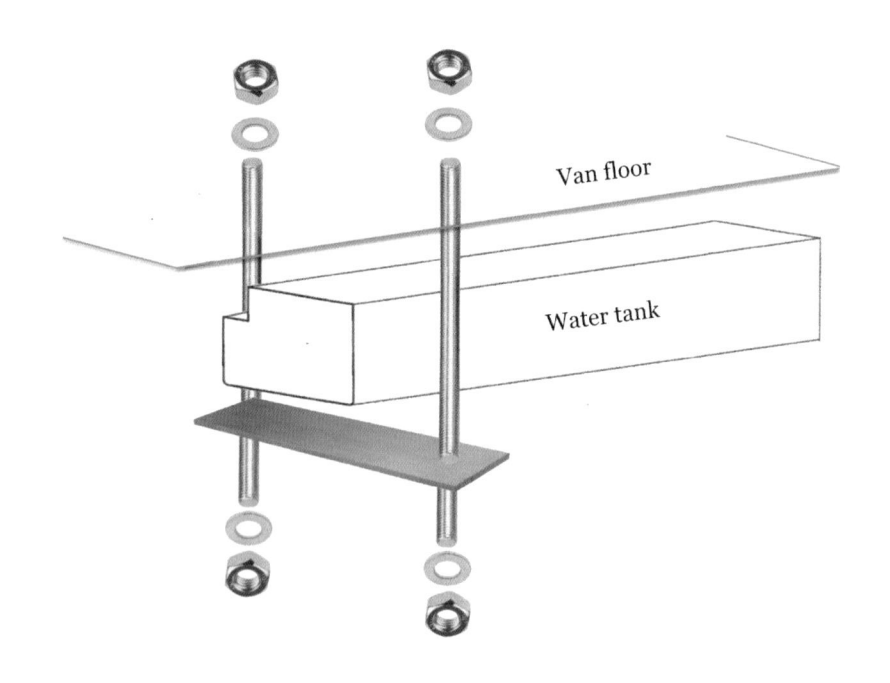

Day 7: Grey Water Tank

Now that you've successfully installed your fresh water tank underneath the van, why not secure the grey water tank?

Grey water tanks are typically smaller than fresh water tanks since you can empty them regularly. We recommend using a water tank sender arm and gauge to monitor the water level so you can know when you need to empty it.

SUPPLIES NEEDED

Item	Qty	Picture
Grey Water Tank This tank will contain your grey water - the water that will drain out of your sink and indoor shower.	1	
M10 Threaded Stainless Steel Rod This metal rod will be used to fix your water tanks underneath the van. You can use a metal grinder to cut it to size.	4	
M10 Stainless Steel Washer This washer will be placed before the nut to ensure the rod is secured in place.	8	
M10 Stainless Steel Lock Nut Make sure to buy the "Lock Nut" type to make sure the rod stays secured even when the van vibrates as you're driving.	8	
Aluminium Flat bar Make sure it's at least 3 mm x 10mm so it can sustain the weight of your tank when full	1	

Water Tank Sender Arm (optional) A tank sender probe is installed into the side of the water tank, then simply connected to the gauge inside the van to monitor the water level in your tanks.	1	
12 mm Pipe - Clear We used this pipe for the water "overflow" or "breather" pipe but you can use 12mm John Guest Pipe if you'd like.	1m	
Screw In Outlet Breather Make sure you get the right size to fit your tank hole and breather pipe.	1	
Mesh Screen (optional) You can tape a little piece of mesh screen at the tip of your overflow pipe to avoid insects getting into your tanks.	1m	
Pipe Retaining Clips These will be used to clip the pipes to the car fuselage.	2	
PVC Pipe Glue Used to secure pipes to their connectors.	1	

Exhaust Heat Wrap (optional) If your water tank is close to your exhaust pipe, we recommend using heat wrap around the exhaust to avoid damages to your tank.	1	

TOOLS NEEDED

Item	Picture
Drill Make sure to get a cordless drill. You'll actually really want to have two to avoid having to switch bits all the time.	
Holesaw Kit I'd recommend buying a couple of holesaw kits for metal and wood as you'll need various sizes throughout the build. You can return the ones you haven't used after you're done!	
Plastic Pipe Cutter Used to cut all your water pipes. A clean cut is required to avoid leaks.	
Metal Grinder Used to cut metal sheets and plates.	
Plumber's Thread Tape Helps avoid leaks when sealing water pipes. Place the end of the plumber's tape on the thread of the pipe and hold it in place with a finger. Wrap the tape around the pipe in the opposite direction to the direction the pipe will be turned.	
Wrench Used for various purposes during your build.	

STEP-BY-STEP GUIDE

Step 1: Repeat the same steps as for securing the fresh water tank in place.

Step 2: Here you can see that the car exhaust is close to the water tank so we used heat wrap and secure it with metal zip ties

Day 8: Plumbing Part 1

Plumbing may seem overwhelming… but it's actually pretty easy and fun! We've designed most of our plumbing using "push fit" or "John Guest" fittings. These work perfectly for both cold and hot water systems and are easy to install even with zero experience.

We'll guide you through each step of the plumbing, starting with the fresh water system, then the grey water.

SUPPLIES NEEDED

Item	Qty	Picture
12V Fresh Water Auto Pump Make sure you read reviews on the pump you select. Select a low noise, high flow pump.	1	
Inline Water Filter This filter should be installed onto the inlet side of the pump.	1	
Mains Water Inlet, Pressure Regulator This will be fixed to the side wall of your van to allow for easy filling of your fresh water tank using a hose.	1	
Water, Brass Adapter (optional) This will allow you to clip on a hose to the USA style water inlets with thread. The clip on system is standard Australian style -- check what's standard in your country of adventure.	1	
Water Heater (optional) We've opted for an electric hot water heater. It's 10L and runs on 12 volts.	1	

Water Pipe, 12mm John Guest, Semi-Rigid Push-In, Blue This flexible but firm water pipe is ideal for campervan installations. Use blue for cold water.	15m	
Water Pipe, 12mm John Guest, Semi-Rigid Push-In, Red This flexible but firm water pipe is ideal for campervan installations. Use red for hot water.	15m	
12mm John Guest Push-On, To 1/2 Inch Male BSP Fits most standard taps and water pumps.	3	
12mm John Guest Push-On, To 1/2 Inch Female BSP Fits most standard taps and water pumps.	6	
One-Way Valve This valve has 12mm John Guest push-on fittings and allows flow in one direction only.	1	
Hot Water Pipe Support Insert These inserts slide into 12mm pipe, before the pipe end is inserted into the push-on fittings. They are required for hot water pipes only.	4	
Locking Clips These locking clips fit 12mm push-on fittings. These prevent pipes from	30	

coming apart after they've been locked in place.		
Push-On Elbow 12mm John Guest, push-on elbow to join two sections of 12mm pipe at a 90 degree angle.	8	
Push-On Tee 12mm John Guest, push-on Tee to join 3 x 12mm pipes together.	1	

TOOLS NEEDED

Item	Picture
Drill Make sure to get a cordless drill. You'll actually really want to have two to avoid having to switch bits all the time.	
Holesaw Kit I'd recommend buying a couple of holesaw kits for metal and wood as you'll need various sizes throughout the build. You can return the ones you haven't used after you're done!	
Plastic Pipe Cutter Used to cut all your water pipes. A clean cut is required to avoid leaks.	
Plumber's Thread Tape Helps avoid leaks when sealing water pipes. Place the end of the plumber's tape on the thread of the pipe and hold it in place with a finger. Wrap the tape around the pipe in the opposite direction to the direction the pipe will be turned.	
Wrench Used for various purposes during your build.	

STEP-BY-STEP GUIDE

Step 1: First, install the Main Water Inlet (used to fill the tank with water using a hose). This should be installed on the outside of the campervan wall, as close as possible to the fresh water tank. To install it, follow the instructions on the manual. You'll need to drill a hole using a holesaw, and then add some Sikaflex to secure it to the van wall.

Attach a 12 mm John Guest Push-On, to 1/2in Female BSB to the Main Water Inlet. Use plumber's tape around the thread.

Then, connect the Main Water Inlet to the Fresh Water Tank Water Inlet, using 12mm blue pipe and elbow connectors as needed.

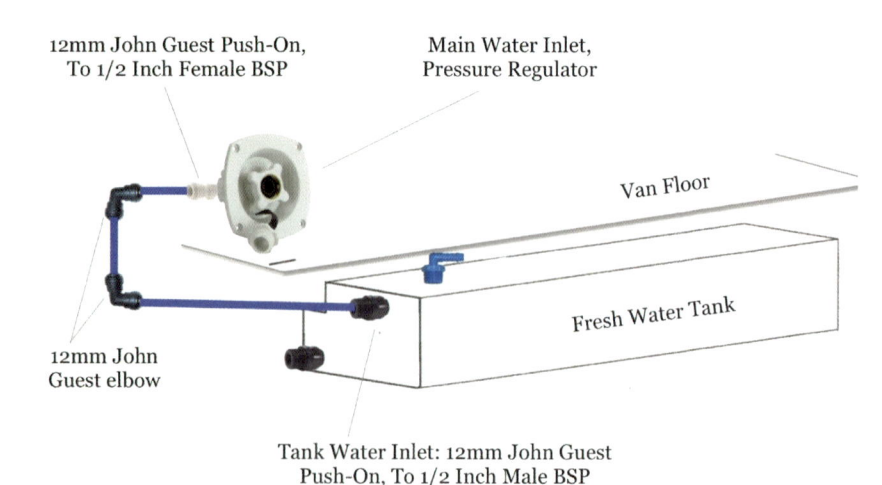

12mm John Guest Push-On, To 1/2 Inch Female BSP

Main Water Inlet, Pressure Regulator

Van Floor

Fresh Water Tank

12mm John Guest elbow

Tank Water Inlet: 12mm John Guest Push-On, To 1/2 Inch Male BSP

Step 2: Insert a 12mm John Guest Push-On, to 1/2in Male BSP connector in the Fresh Water Tank Water Outlet. Use plumber's tape.

Secure the water pump to the car fuselage, then connect the Tank Water Outlet to the Water Filter then the Water Pump. It's very important to have the water filter in between the water outlet and the pump. If you don't add a water filter, your pump can get damaged.

Finally, drill a hole through the van's floor. Make sure the hole is big enough to accomodate the 12mm pipe, as well as electrical wires for the pump and the water level sensors.

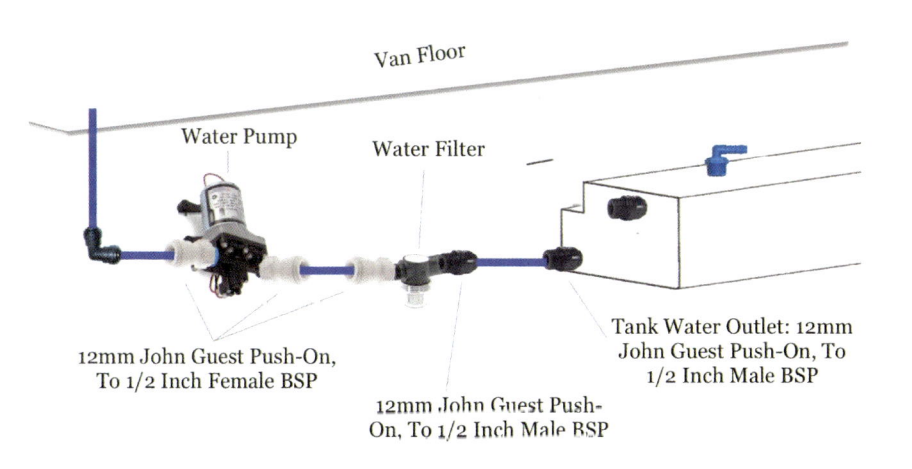

Van Floor

Water Pump

Water Filter

12mm John Guest Push-On, To 1/2 Inch Female BSP

12mm John Guest Push-On, To 1/2 Inch Male BSP

Tank Water Outlet: 12mm John Guest Push-On, To 1/2 Inch Male BSP

Step 3: Set up your water heater. Make sure it is secured to the floor.

Connect the cold water pipe (coming from the tank underneath the van) to the cold water inlet of the water heater using a John Guest Tee. Place an inline one-way valve just before the cold water inlet. You now have cold water coming into your water heater and hot water coming out of it! Make sure you do not turn the water heater on until you have water in your pipes!

Your cold and hot water pipes can now be connected to your sink, indoor shower and outdoor shower. We will get to that later when your shower is close to being completed.

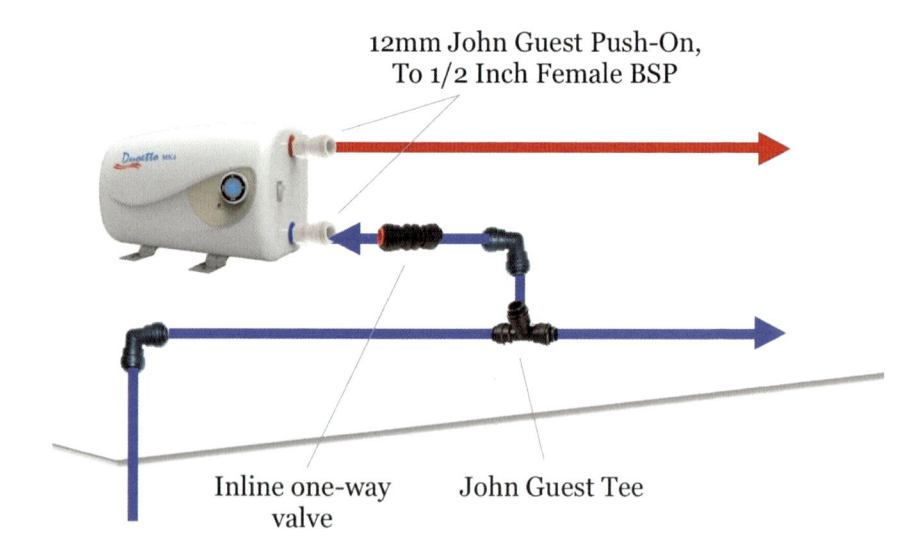

12mm John Guest Push-On, To 1/2 Inch Female BSP

Inline one-way valve

John Guest Tee

Day 9: Electrical System

Today, we'll be putting together all of the electrical components.

This may seem extremely overwhelming, especially if you have no experience with electrical components. But if you've followed our steps to carefully design your electrical system (earlier in this book), it will be a piece of cake.

We will be guiding you through building the electrical system below. Depending on which electrical components you've chosen and decisions you've made, you may need to adjust some steps. However, understanding the process will help you build your custom electrical system.

Before actually connecting any of the parts, we recommend setting down each individual component. Use a solid piece of wood and screw in each component to test your layout.

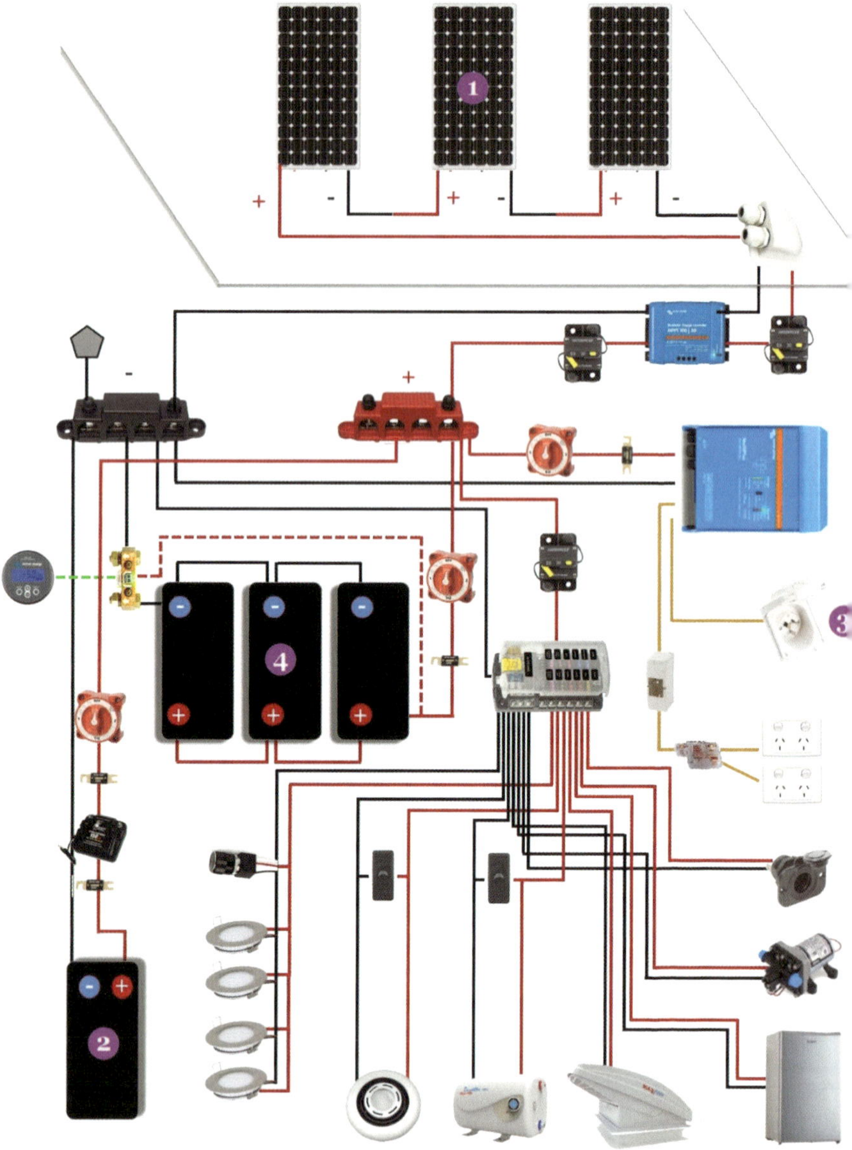
1
+
-
+
-
+
-
-
+
4
2
3

SUPPLIES NEEDED

Item	Qty	Picture
Power Distribution Block - Black Bus Bar A bus bar connects all the terminals together into one "bus." This makes one electrical "node: of the same voltage. This will be to connect all negative wire connections.	1	
Power Distribution Block - Red Bus Bar Same as your Black Bus Bar, but for positive connections.	1	
Circuit Breaker - 30 A 30 amp circuit breaker with manual reset button.	1	
Circuit Breaker - 50 A 50 amp circuit breaker with manual reset button.	1	
Circuit Breaker - 100 A 100 amp circuit breaker with manual reset button.	1	
Fuse - 250 A 250 amp fuse for high current applications.	4	
Fuse Protective Box Protects your high amperage fuses.	4	

On/Off Switch Allows you to switch different parts of your system off.	3	
Solar Controller We opted for the Victron BlueSolar MPPT 100/30 which includes three state charging.	1	
12-Volt AGM Battery We recommend getting 12-volt deep cell batteries because of their good value. Alternatively, you can get Lithium batteries, which perform and last longer but are much more expensive.	3	
Battery Monitor and Shunt Monitors voltage and current of your battery bank and calculates power, state-of-charge, and time-to-go. We opted for the Victron BMV-712 with bluetooth.	1	
Battery Isolator / Alternator This will allow you to charge your battery bank while driving. We recommend purchasing one with a manual override that would allow you to start your car battery using your battery bank in case you accidentally drain your car battery (e.g. by not driving your van frequently enough). We opted for the Battery Doctor 125 Amp/150 Amp Battery Isolator.	1	
Light Switch Allows you to turn your appliances on/off. Used for the shower fan and shower heater.	2	

12-volt DC Dimmer Allows you to create low-light ambiance. Only use for lights.	2	
12-volt DC LED Lights Make sure to use LED lights to use less power. We opted for some with built in spring clips to make installation easier.	10	
12-volt Dash Socket This allows you to plug in different 12-volt appliances, USB chargers, etc. We recommend using this "cigarette lighter" option and add a removable USB plug as it's more versatile and won't get outdated.	2	
Fuse Blocks The fuse blocks consolidate branch circuits and eliminate the tangle of in-line fuses for electronics and other appliances. Their design makes them ideal for campervan (12-volt) DC electrical systems.	1	
Assortment of Fuses Make sure to get 5amp, 10amp, 15amp, 20amp, and 40amp fuses for your various appliances.	20	
Power Inlet Allows you to connect power from outside the van (mains) to charge your battery bank.	1	

Inverter / Charger The "inverter" function will invert 12-volt current from your battery bank to 120V (or 230V) for regular power outlets. The "charger" function allows you to charge your battery bank using an external power outlet. We opted for a Victron 80/30 MultiPlus Compact but other cheaper models are likely a better value.	1	
High Voltage Circuit Breaker 120-volt (or 230-volt depending on your country). We opted for a DIY system that allows you to build a high-voltage system without a professional. If you don't, please hire a pro to install your high-voltage system.	1	
Breaker Box This goes on top of your circuit breaker to protect it.	1	
Double Power Point 120-volt (or 230-volt, depending on your country). We opted for a DIY system that allows you to build a high-voltage system without a professional. If you don't, hire a pro.	2	
High Voltage Interconnecting Cables 120-volt (or 230-volt depending on your country). We opted for a DIY system that allows you to build a high-voltage system without a professional. If you don't, hire a pro.	2	

High Voltage Double Adapter Takes one 120-volt (or 230-volt) Inlet and splits it into two 120-volt (or 230-volt) outlets. We opted for a DIY system that allows you to build a high-voltage system without a professional. If you don't, hire a pro.	1	
Wire Joiners Make sure to get 2.5mm and 4mm joiners.	50	
Lugs - various sizes Make sure you get 2.5 mm, 4mm, and 2.0 Gauge lugs (for your battery cables).	30	
Cable Heat Shrink Tubes (optional) Used to protect wire connections from damage, water, and heat. Alternatively, you can use electrical tape.		
Solar Cable - 6mm² This cable is ideal for connecting your outdoor solar panels to your solar regulator. They're UV protected.	5m	
2 Gauge Battery Cable This is for connecting your batteries together.	2m	
Twin Cable - 4mm, 15 amp This low amperage cable is ideal for connecting all your 12-volt systems (lights, fans, fridge, etc.).	5m	

Twin & Earth Cable - 2.5 mm This cable will be used for connecting your high voltage (i.e. regular) plugs.	2m

TOOLS NEEDED

Item	Picture
Drill Make sure to get a cordless drill (or two)!	
Holesaw Kit We'd recommend buying a couple of holesaw kits for metal and wood as you'll need various sizes throughout the build. You can return the ones you haven't used after you're done!	
Electrical Tape This will help you finish connections and hold wires together, among other things.	
Wire Striper and Crimper This will be needed to cut, strip and crimp all your wires.	
Battery Cable Lug Crimper Hammer (optional) This will allow you to crimp large battery cables. You will need this only if your wire crimper doesn't allow for large cables.	

STEP-BY-STEP GUIDE

Step 1: We'll start by connecting the Solar Panels to your electrical system. Use 6mm² solar cable for this.

Connect the negative solar cable (coming from the solar panels on your roof) to the negative solar (PV-) connector of the Solar Controller. Then, connect the positive solar cable (coming from the solar panels on your roof) to a 30 Amp circuit breaker then to the positive solar (PV+) connector of the Solar Controller. Make sure your 30 Amp circuit breaker is disconnected at this stage. Only connect it when you've connected your battery bank.

Next, connect the Solar Controller to the bus bars. Connect the negative Battery (BATT -) connector of the Solar Connector to the Negative Bus Bar directly. Then, connect the positive Battery (BATT +) connector of the Solar Connector to a 50 Amp circuit breaker then to to the Positive Bus Bar.

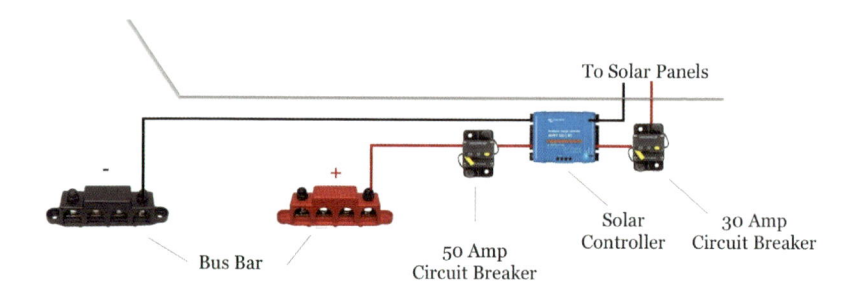

Step 2: We'll now install your battery bank and connect it to your electrical system. Use 2.0 Gauge battery cable and lugs for this step.

Install your 12-volt batteries in parallel. This way, the voltage will remain 12-volt throughout. Connect the negative poles of the batteries together. Repeat with the positive poles. Make sure the positive and negative cables don't touch each other to avoid a short circuit (and a big, scary spark).

Next, connect the positive bus bar to an On/Off switch, then to a 250-amp Fuse, then to the Positive pole of your last battery bank.

Important note: Your batteries are heavy and need to be property fixed to the van's floor. Make sure to build a secure encasing for your batteries with wood and screws.

Next, connect the negative bus bar to the shunt, then to the negative pole of your first battery. Finally, connect the negative bus bar to the car fuselage (i.e "ground"). You can simply drill a small hole in the car fuselage, then wrap your wire through the hole and secure it in place using a bolt and nut. Note: the purpose of connecting an electrical system to the "ground" is to limit the voltage imposed by lightning events or contact with higher voltage lines. This is just a precaution.

Additionally, connect the shunt to your monitoring system (if applicable) using the provided cable (Green dotted line. This cable will come with the shunt). Also, your shunt will likely require a cable from the shunt to the positive of your battery bank (Red dotted line. This cable will come with your shunt).

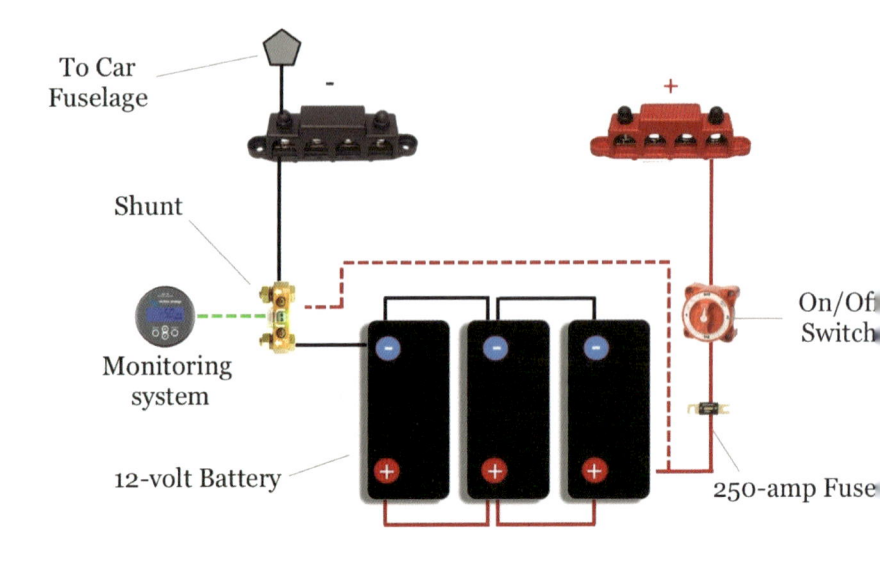

To Car Fuselage

Shunt

Monitoring system

12-volt Battery

On/Off Switch

250-amp Fuse

Step 3: We'll now connect the Battery Bank to the car battery so that you can charge your battery bank while driving. Use 2.0 Gauge battery cable and lugs for this step.

Connect the positive Bus Bar to an On/Off switch, then to a 250-amp fuse, then to the Battery Isolator Auxiliary (AUX +) Connector. Then, connect the Battery Isolator Main (MAIN+) Connector to a 250-Amp Fuse, then to the positive pole of the car battery. Connect the black wire from the battery isolator to the negative bus bar. Alternatively, if your isolator doesn't come with a negative wire, connect a 2.0 Gauge battery cable from the negative pole of the car battery to the negative Bus Bar. (Note: this will reduce voltage drop due to the car fuselage in case your car battery is far from your battery bank.)

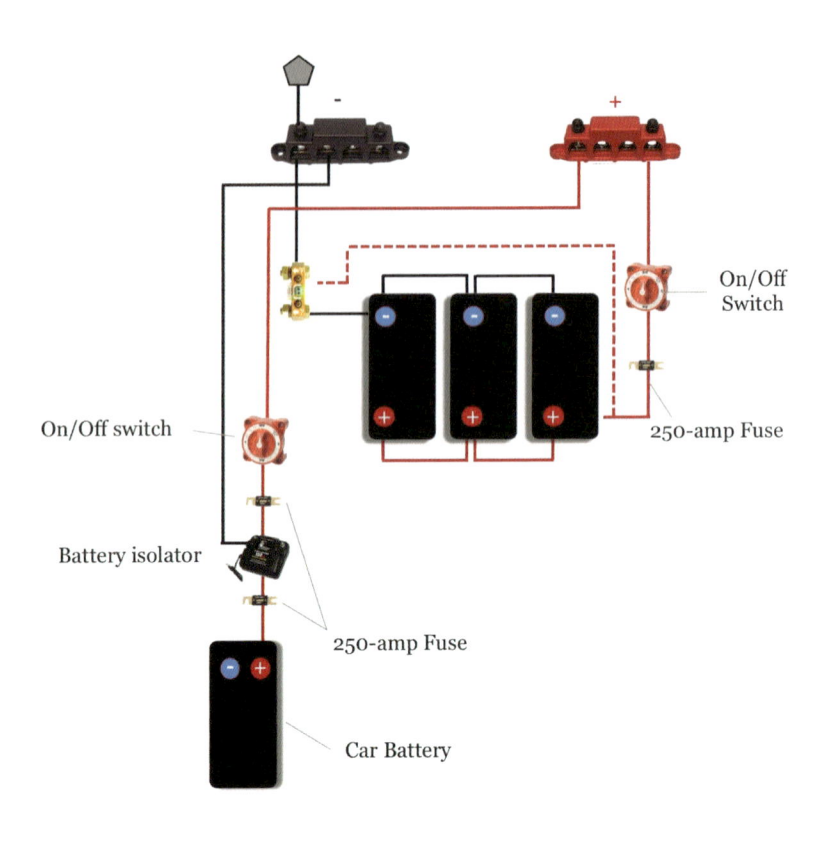

On/Off
Switch

250-amp Fuse

On/Off switch

Battery isolator

250-amp Fuse

Car Battery

Step 4: Next, we'll set up the high voltage portion of the system (120-volts or 230-volts depending on your country). In most countries, it is not legal to install this system without a professional. There are some DIY high-voltage systems for campervans that exist. We opted for this in our build. If you don't, please consult a professional.

Connect the Positive Bus Bar (red) to an On/Off Switch, then a 250-Amp Fuse, then to the Positive DC (DC+) Connector of the Inverter/Charger. Use 2.0 Gauge battery cable and lugs for this step.

Connect the Negative Bus Bar (black) to the negative DC (DC-) Connector of the Inverter/Charger. Use 2.0 Gauge battery cable and lugs for this step.

Install the Power Inlet to the wall of your campervan by cutting the appropriate sized hole using your hole saw kit. Use Sikaflex to make sure it's waterproof. Connect the Power Inlet to the high-voltage IN port of the Inverter / Charger.

Finally, connect the high-voltage OUT port of the Inverter / Charger to the high-voltage Circuit Breaker, then the Adapter and Power Points. Use the provided cables from your DIY kit for this step.

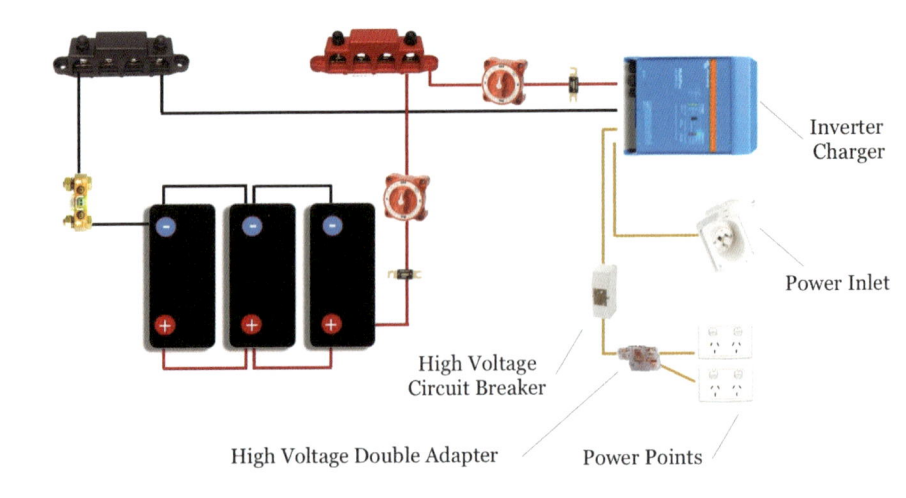

Inverter Charger

Power Inlet

High Voltage Circuit Breaker

High Voltage Double Adapter

Power Points

Step 5: We'll now connect the 12-volt DC Fuse Blocks to your main system. We'll then connect all 12-volt DC Outlets to it. Use Twin Cable - 4mm, 15 amp for this step.

First, connect the Negative Bus Bar to the negative pole of the Fuse Blocks. Then Connect the Positive Bus Bar to a 100-amp Circuit Breaker, then to the positive pole of the Fuse Blocks. Make sure your 100-amp Circuit Breaker is disconnected at this stage.

Then, connect all your appliances, lights, plugs, fans, etc. to your Fuse Blocks using the appropriate negative and positive poles. Refer to individual manuals to select the appropriate fuse for each. We recommend also recording somewhere what each fuse is, in case you ever need that information down the line :).

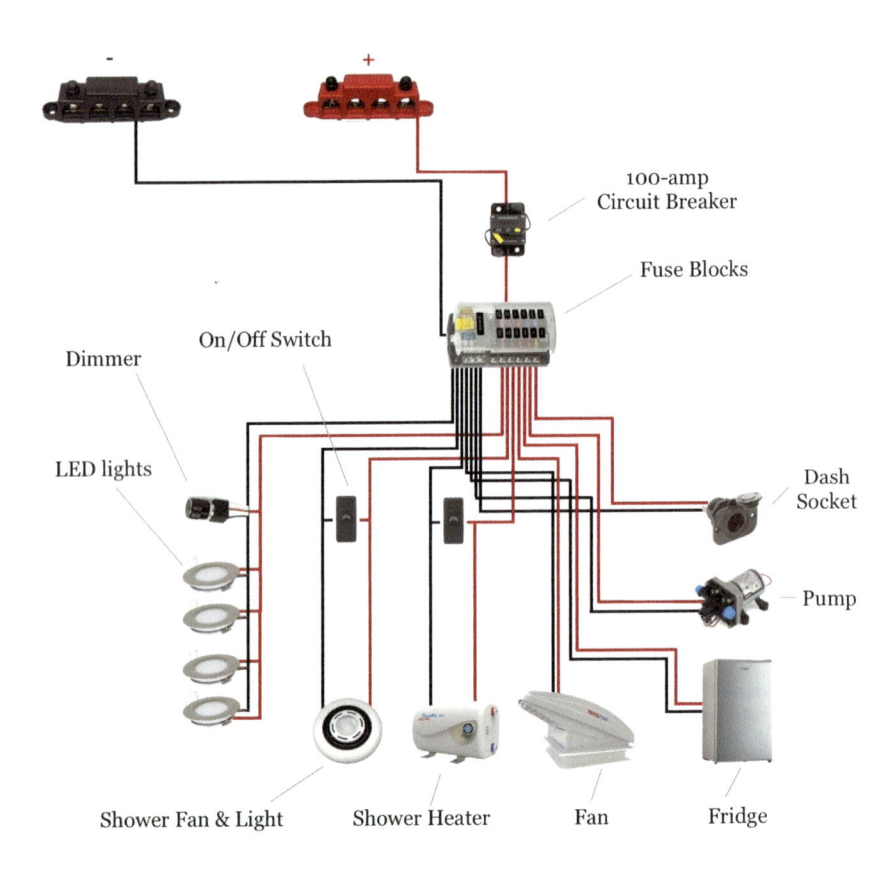

100-amp Circuit Breaker

Fuse Blocks

Dimmer

On/Off Switch

LED lights

Dash Socket

Pump

Shower Fan & Light

Shower Heater

Fan

Fridge

That's it! You've now completed your electrical system. It's ready to be turned live. Simply connect the Circuit Breaker and Switches ON, and you're ready to roll. Congratulations!

Day 10: Ceiling - Insulation & Framing

Let's now tackle insulation and framing for the roof.

Similar to the wall insulation, we selected glasswool, a.k.a sheep wool, because of its great thermal noise-canceling properties. Make sure to wear safety goggles, mask, and gloves, as well as a long-sleeve shirt, to avoid coming into contact with small glass particles (you're probably all too familiar if you didn't listen to us the first time).

For the framing, we've selected shiplap, a kind of wooden board that's often used for constructing sheds, barns, and other rustic buildings. It has a groove cut into the top and bottom, which allows the pieces to fit together snugly, forming a tight seal. We really love the finished look of shiplap for a campervan. It feels very cozy yet clean. It's also easier to install than giant pieces of plywood. We'll be using 4.8 meter long shiplap boards that cover the full length of the campervan.

SUPPLIES NEEDED

Item	Qty	Picture
Insulation Glasswood We opted for this insulation made of recycled glass and sand because it improves acoustic and thermal performance and is extremely easy to install in a van.	40m²	
Shiplap - 4.8 meters Solid shiplap pine lining boards are a great choice for lining interior walls and ceilings.	24	
Timber screws Use 25mm to 45mm timber screw to screw plywood together and to the van walls / ceiling.	100	

TOOLS NEEDED

Item	Picture
Drill Make sure to get a cordless drill. You'll actually really want to have two to avoid having to switch bits all the time.	
Utility Knife You'll use this to cut the wool.	
Jigsaw A jigsaw will help you cut any boards that need a non-straight edge, to fit your van.	
Mitre Saw This will be used to cut your shiplap to the correct length.	
Holesaw Kit This will be to cut holes for your lights into your shiplap.	
Safety Gloves Important to wear when handling insulation wool and sharp metal.	

Safety Mask Important to wear when handling insulation wool or cutting metal parts.	
Safety Goggles Important to wear when handling insulation wool or cutting metal parts.	

STEP-BY-STEP GUIDE

Step 1: Start with the center of your roof. Cut the first shiplap to the right length (using your mitre saw). Drill holes (using your holesaw kit) for your light fixtures. Fix the first shiplap to the roof drilling into the existing metal frames.

Step 2: After you've fixed two or three shiplaps to the roof, cut the insulation glasswool to the correct size and thread it through your first couple pieces of shiplap, which will help keep it in place. Make sure the electrical wires go between the insulation and the shiplap boards, not between the insulation and your metal roof.

Step 3: Once you reach the corners, you will need to use your jigsaw to cut the shiplap at various angles to fit properly and flush. Additionally, you will need some cuts around your fans. This will likely require a few "re-do's," and lots of fine tuning.

Step 4: Once you've finished the roof, you may also decide to cover the walls of your van using shiplap (like we did, shortly after this photo was taken).

Day 11: Hanging Cabinets

Now that you've completed your ceiling, you can build hanging cabinets. These are great for storing your clothes, food, etc.

We're not big fans of having to build cabinets when you can buy great prefabricated ones. Kitchen cabinets that sit on the floor are great examples of things you can buy premade. However, since the hanging cabinets will be hanging from the top corners of vans, which don't typically have straight corners or edges, you'll need to build these frames custom. You can use standard doors, however.

SUPPLIES NEEDED

Item	Qty	Picture
Timber Pine Use standard timber pine to build the frame. 20mmx40mmx2.4m pine works well for hanging cabinets.	20	
2440x1220x6mm Structural Plywood This will form the edges of your cabinets.	2	
Cabinet Doors Typically 300mm or 400mm height, depending on your needs.	8	
Cabinet Hinge Pack We recommend getting gas struts to hold your doors open when desired.	8	
Angle Brackets Use a variety of angle brackets to support your timber frames.	30	
Batten screws Use 45mm to 65mm batten screws to screw structural wood together.	100	
Timber screws Use 25mm to 45mm timber screws to screw plywood together.	100	

TOOLS NEEDED

Item	Picture
Drill Make sure to get a cordless drill. You'll actually really want to have two to avoid having to switch bits all the time.	
Jigsaw This will be crucial for making your cabinets fit.	
Mitre Saw This wil cut your straight structural timbers.	
Holesaw Kit This will make the holes for your hinges and gas struts, as well as the lights under your cabinets, if using.	
Leveler A leveler will help you make sure you frames are angled correctly.	
Measuring tape For this project, be sure to measure twice, cut once.	

STEP-BY-STEP GUIDE

Step 1: Use timber pine to build the frame for your hanging cabinets. Use angle brackets to reinforce your cabinets. Make sure you build these the correct size to accommodate your prefab doors, if using.

Step 2: Use a tape and leveler to make sure your frame has straight angles. Use timber to separate each cabinet so you can fix doors.

Step 3: Repeat on both sides of your van.

Step 4: Build bottom covers for your cabinets using plywood. Drill holes for the lights and wire them. Test your lights before adding another layer of plywood inside the bottom of each cabinet (so that your clothes sit on top of that, rather than on top of electrical wires).

Step 5: Add doors using hinges. We strongly recommend adding gas struts so that doors can be held open when desired.

Step 6: Most likely the length of your van won't be an exact multiple of door length. In our case, we left a small opening in between the cabinets on one side. We added a piece of wood (from our kitchen countertops) to house a small indoor plant.

Step 7: Similarly, at the end of other hanging cabinets we added a triangular-shaped piece of wood to house another plant.

Day 12: Shower Tray & Fan

In the next couple of days, we will tackle the rest of the indoor shower build.

First, we'll add the shower drain so we can fix the shower tray in place.

Then, we'll add the shower fan/light combo to the roof.

SUPPLIES NEEDED

Item	Qty	Picture
12V Extractor Fan with Halogen Light Ideal for campervan showers. Light and fan have separate wires, so can be connected together or independently to a switch.	1	
Aluminium Roof Cowl This outer section sits on the roof, providing a waterproof vent.	1	
Waste Fitting Suits 25mm drain hose and plug. Fits a 35mm hole.	1	
PVC Black hose - 25mm This will be used for your waste plumbing (from your sink and shower to your grey water tank).	1m	
PVC Pipe Glue Used to secure pipes to their connectors.	1	
Hose Clamps These will be used to secure your 25mm waste water pipes.	1	

| Sikaflex Pro
Get more than you think you might need -- trust us. | 5 | |

TOOLS NEEDED

Item	Picture
Drill Make sure to get a cordless drill. You'll actually really want to have two to avoid having to switch bits all the time.	
Holesaw Kit Make sure you have a large metal one that will fit the holes needed for your shower light/fan, as well as your shower drain.	
Caulk Gun This low cost tool will help you distribute silicone, gap filler & adhesive cartridges easily.	
Wrench Used for various purposes during your build.	

STEP-BY-STEP GUIDE

Step 1: Drill a hole in your shower tray and van floor for the waste fitting. Make sure the hole can accommodate a 25mm pipe and doesn't interfere with any of the car pipes underneath the van.

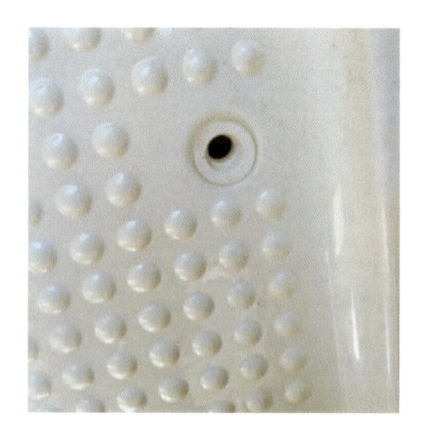

Step 2: Secure the water fitting to the shower tray. Use Sikaflex on both sides to make sure it's waterproof.

Step 3: Secure a 25mm PVC pipe through the floor's hole and glue the end of the pipe to the waste fitting, using PVC glue. Use a hose clamp to further secure the hose.

Step 4: Use Sikaflex to fix the shower tray to the floor. Make sure your electrical wires (if any, in our case we had the fridge and car battery wires) go through the sides of the tray and now underneath.

Step 5: Drill a hole through the roof to accommodate the shower fan/light.

Step 6: Wire and test the fan. Then fix the fan using the provided screws and Sikaflex to make sure everything is waterproof. Add the roof cowl to the roof using Sikaflex.

Day 13: Shower Wet Panels & Framing

Today, you'll be finishing your indoor shower! You will be adding the shower wet panels to make the inside of the shower waterproof.

And finally, you'll finish framing the outside of the shower wall and add a door. We're not going to lie, this was one of the hardest steps for us, but nothing you can't handle with a little patience and a good attitude. We'll guide you through it all!

SUPPLIES NEEDED

Item	Qty	Picture
Wet Area Wall Panels: 2400mmx1200mm Ideal for the lining of walls in wet areas such as bathrooms. We opted for these instead of individual tiles due to stronger resistance to vibrations as we drive.	3	
Linear Wet Area Internal Corner Joiner These are an external corner moulding to connect two wet area panels together.	4	
Linear Wet Area Panel Ends These are a PVC joiner for use at the ends of wet area panels.	2	
Retractable Shower Screen A compact and lightweight shower screen ideal for confined spaces such as caravans or motor-homes.	1	
Sikaflex Pro Trust us -- get an extra or two, which you can return later.	5	

TOOLS NEEDED

Item	Picture
Drill Make sure to get a cordless drill. You'll actually really want to have two to avoid having to switch bits all the time.	
Jigsaw Your jigsaw will be your best friend on this job. Be sure to use blades intended for metal for this project.	
Clamps Use to hold your bits together while they're drying.	
Caulk Gun This low cost tool will help you distribute silicone, gap filler & adhesive cartridges easily.	

STEP-BY-STEP GUIDE

Step 1: Measure and cut the wet area panels for the shower walls and ceiling using a Jigsaw. Make sure to accommodate for the corner joiners (where two panels intersect) and ends (where the panels meet the shower tray). Enlist a friend, and try to put all of the panels into place at the same time to ensure they fit. Use Sikaflex to glue the walls and ceiling. You likely want to start with the back wall and work your way forward on either side, leaving the ceiling piece for last. Then use clamps (or wedge in pieces of wood) to secure the panels and hold them while they dry. You will need at least 2 people for this job, so make sure you get help for this step -- trust us!

Step 8: Then, Sikaflex the sides of all panels to ensure they are waterproof. Also be sure to sikaflex along the bottom where your wall panels meet your shower tray.

Step 9: Once your panels are dry, you can install the shower door. Follow the instructions on the shower door manual, as all are different. Make sure to use Sikaflex to waterproof it.

Step 10: Finally, you can finish the outside shower wall using shiplap.

Day 14: Plumbing - Part 2

We will now tackle the rest of the plumbing. Now that the shower walls are in place, you will be able to hook up the shower mixer and shower head.

We will also lay out the plumbing for the outdoor shower (if you choose to have one) and sink. It's easier to do this step before setting up the kitchen cabinet and sofa.

SUPPLIES NEEDED

Item	Qty	Picture
Shower Mixer This will be connected to your hot and cold shower pipes. It controls the mix of hot and cold water.	1	
Shower Hose and Bar This connects to your shower mixer and shower head. This will likely come with a shower head, but we replaced ours with one that uses less warter.	1	
Shower Head We recommend the Oxygenics RV Shower Head because it mixes air into the line to provide better water pressure with less water usage.	1	
Water Pipe, 12mm John Guest, Semi-Rigid Push-In, Blue This flexible but firm water pipe is ideal for campervan installations. Use blue for cold water.	5m	
Water Pipe, 12mm John Guest, Semi-Rigid Push-In, Red This flexible but firm water pipe is ideal for campervan installations. Use red for hot water.	5m	

12mm John Guest Push-On, To 1/2 Inch Female BSP Fits most standard taps and water pumps.	8	
Hot Water Pipe Support Insert These inserts slide into 12mm pipe, before the pipe end is inserted into the push-on fittings. They are required for hot water pipes only.	15	
Locking Clips These locking clips fit 12mm push-on fittings. These prevent pipes from coming apart.	30	
Push-On Elbow 12mm John Guest, push-on elbow to join two sections of 12mm at 90 degrees.	5	
Push-On Tee 12mm John Guest, push-on Tee to join 3 x 12mm pipes together.	4	
PVC Black hose - 25mm This will be used for your waste plumbing (from your sink and shower to your grey water tank).	10m	
25mm Elbow 25mm barb elbow to join two sections of 25mm pipe at 90 degrees.	1	

25mm Tee 25mm barb Tee to join 3 x 25mm pipes together.	1	
25mm One-way valve This valve has 25mm barb fittings and allows flow in one direction only.	1	
Hepvo Valve These valves prevent backflow of air and water into showers and sinks. Make sure you get adequate fittings to connect it to your grey water pipe	1	
Threaded Hose Barb 25mm x 1in BSP fitting These will be used to connect the 25mm grey water pipes to your grey water tank.	2	
25mm Inline Tap Barbed Valve This will be used to drain your grey water when needed.	1	
PVC Pipe Glue Used to secure pipes to their connectors.	1	
Hose Clamps These will be used to secure your 25mm waste water pipes.	14	

Shiplap - 4.8 meters Solid shiplap pine lining boards are a great choice for lining interior walls and ceilings.	2	
2440x1220x6mm Structural Plywood This plywood for walls and cabinets.	1	

TOOLS NEEDED

Item	Picture
Drill Make sure to get a cordless drill. You'll actually really want to have two to avoid having to switch bits all the time.	
Jigsaw A jigsaw will help you tackle intricate and curved cuts in timber or steel. Given that nothing in a van is straight, this is a must have tool!	
Holesaw Kit I'd recommend buying a couple of holesaw kits for metal and wood as you'll need various sizes throughout the build. You can return the ones you haven't used after you're done!	
Plastic Pipe Cutter Used to cut all your water pipes. A clean cut is required to avoid leaks.	
Plumber's Thread Tape Helps avoid leaks when sealing water pipes. Place the end of the plumber's tape on the thread of the pipe and hold it in place with a finger. Wrap the tape around the pipe in the opposite direction to the direction the pipe will be turned.	

Wrench Used for various purposes during your build.	

STEP-BY-STEP GUIDE

Step 1: First connect John Guest Tees for hot and cold pipes going to your outdoor shower (if you're adding one). In our case, our outdoor shower is on the opposite side of our main plumbing so the plumbing goes through the base of our sofa. You may need several pairs of John Guest elbows to direct the pipes exactly where you need them.

Next, connect John Guest Tees for hot and cold pipes going to your sink. The sink tap will most likely come with hot and cold water flexible pipes to connect 12mm John Guest Push-on to ½ in female BSP.

Next, use John Guest elbows to direct the pipes to your indoor shower tap.

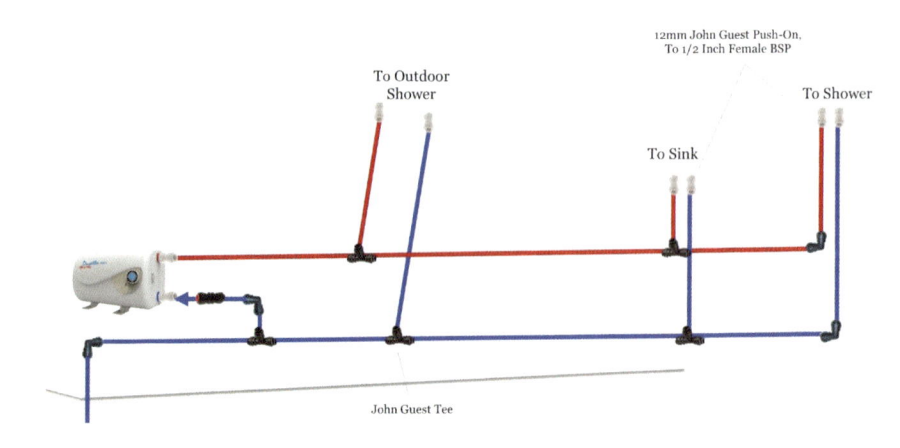

Step 2: Install your shower mixer. You will need to drill a hole through your shower's wall. Follow the shower mixer manual instructions. Use a small piece of wall to fix the mixer to the wall. Sikaflex from the inside of the shower to make sure it's waterproof. Connect the shower pipes to your shower mixer. Then connect your shower mixer to the shower hose and head. You'll likely need several John Guest elbows.

12mm John Guest Push-On, To 1/2 Inch Female BSP

Shower Mixer

Step 3: Next, we'll be setting up the grey water plumbing. This will go from your shower drain and sink drain to your grey water tank. In our case, the grey water tank is underneath the van (to maximize space). Use 25mm black flexible PVC pipe for this. For each connection, use PVC glue as well as hose clamps.

First connect the PVC pipe from your shower drain to a 25mm elbow, then to a 25mm one-way valve. Then, connect it to a 25mm Tee to go to the sink tap. You may not have the sink in place yet at this stage, but plan carefully where this pipe should go and drill a hole through the floor to accommodate for it.

Continue connecting the grey water pipe towards the grey water tank. Connect a Hepvo valve after the 25mm tee.

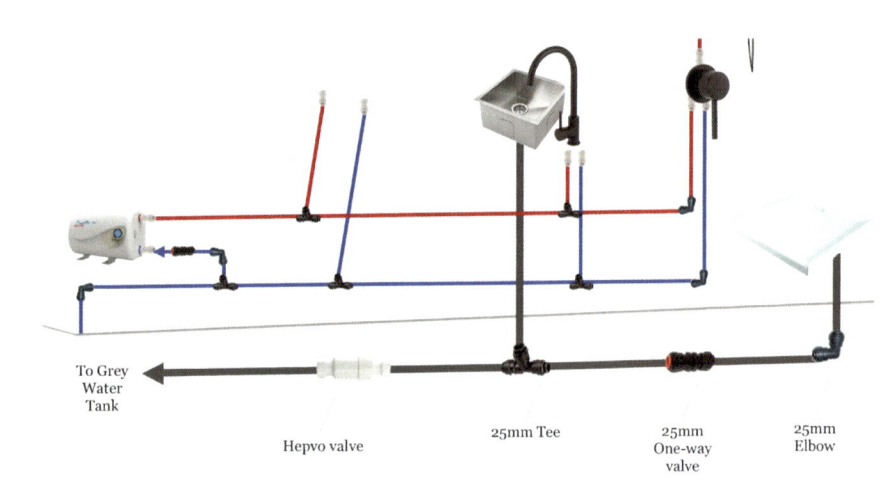

174

Step 4: Connect the grey water pipe to the grey water tank inlet using a threaded hose barb 25mm x 1in BSP fitting.

Then, connect the grey water tank outlet to another piece of grey water pipe then to an inline tap. You want to make sure the tap is easily accessible to empty your grey water tank when needed. For each connection, use PVC glue as well as hose clamps

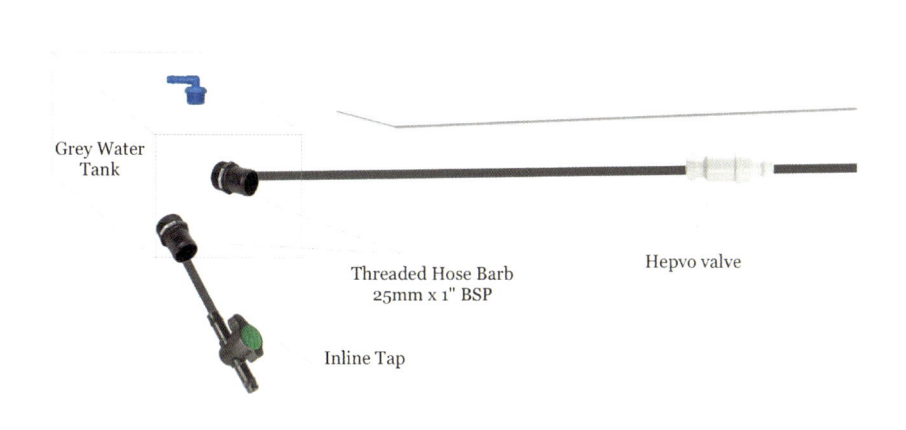

Grey Water Tank

Threaded Hose Barb 25mm x 1" BSP

Hepvo valve

Inline Tap

That's it, your plumbing is done! You'll just have to connect the sink tap and outdoor shower when you install them!

Once you've finished the plumbing you can finish the shower side wall that houses all the pipes and electrical.

Step 1: Cut a piece of plywood for the outside wall of the shower (to house all pipes and electrical). Cut holes for the various plugs, switches, dimmers, water level monitor and battery monitor (this will depend on your layout / electrical needs).

Step 2: Repeat the same holes on shiplap (if you're covering your wall with it)

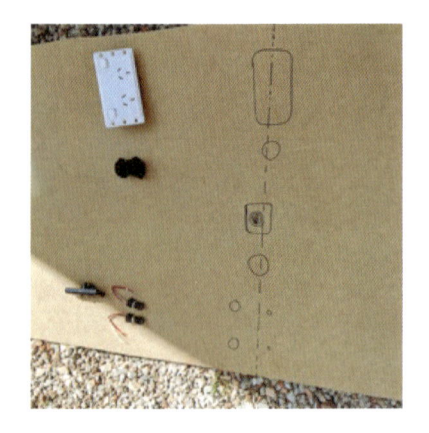

Step 3: Fix the plywood and shiplap to the wall. Make sure to test all electronics (and plumbing) before fully fixing this wall. Note that plugs and switches here are covered with painter's tape in anticipation of painting the shiplap.

Step 4: Finish covering the wall with shiplap.

Day 15: Outdoor shower

Installing the outdoor shower, once you've done all the plumbing, is actually extremely easy.

First, you'll cut yet another hole into your campervan's wall. By now, you must be used to doing it so it will be a piece of cake.

Then, we'll set up the outdoor shower box set, connect it to our cold and hot water pipes, and viola! Within a few hours you'll have your outdoor shower ready.

SUPPLIES NEEDED

Item	Qty	Picture
Exterior Shower Box Set Hand Held Sprayer Holder We opted for a shower box set making it extremely easy to add an outside shower to your set up.	1	
Sikaflex Pro Make sure you buy it in whatever color your van is or use clear.	5	

TOOLS NEEDED

Item	Picture
Drill Make sure to get a cordless drill. You'll actually really want to have two to avoid having to switch bits all the time.	
Jigsaw This is what you'll use to cut your hole in the campervan wall.	
Metal grinder You may also opt to use this to cut the hole in your campervan wall.	
Caulk Gun This low cost tool will help you distribute silicone, gap filler & adhesive cartridges easily.	
Electrical Tape Just used to mark where you'll cut your hole, so can be any color.	
Plumber's Thread Tape Helps avoid leaks when sealing water pipes.	

Wrench
Used for various purposes during your build

STEP-BY-STEP GUIDE

Step 1: Mark the van's wall using electrical tape. Refer to the shower instruction manual for the exact dimensions. Use the jigsaw or metal grinder to cut the hole.

Step 2: Make sure the hole goes through the plywood (or shiplap) on the inside, and is wide enough for you to connect your water pipes.

Step 3: Fix the shower box using the provided screws. Use Sikaflex (after removing the electrical tape) to make sure it's waterproof.

Step 4: Connect your water pipes. Make sure to use plumber's thread tape to avoid leaks.

Step 5: Test your outdoor shower!

Day 16: Bed Frame

Today, you'll be tackling the bed frame.

We chose for our bed frame to be static, as opposed to having a larger couch area that transforms into a bed at night.

We preferred a static bed because we experienced modular layouts in rental campervans before and didn't love having to transform the layout every night. Also, and more importantly, having a static bed allows us to have a ton of storage underneath, which we really need. We have so many things in our storage under the bed: two kitesurfs, a kiteboard, a tent and other camping gear, a dozen spearguns, fins, wetsuits, an inflatable boat, a boat motor and battery, extra diesel, yoga mats, spare water, and so much more.

We also decided to go with a queen bed. Since we have a bit of extra room on one side of the bed, we built a small cabinet alongside the bed. Half of it we use as a "night drawer" with a switch for the lights as well as plugs to charge our phones. The other half we use to house a laundry bag, rain jackets, and other items we need regularly but not daily.

SUPPLIES NEEDED

Item	Qty	Picture
Structural Pine Timber: 35x75mmx2.4m This pine is ideal for framing your shower, bed and sofa.	10	
2440x1220x6mm Structural Plywood This will create a surface for your mattress to sit on.	2	
Batten Screws Use 45mm to 65mm batten screws to screw structural wood together.	100	
Timber screws Use 25mm to 45mm timber screw to screw plywood together.	100	
Angle Brackets Use a variety of angle brackets to support your timber frames.	30	

TOOLS NEEDED

Item	Picture
Drill Big day for the drill -- be sure to have it (or both) charged up!	
Jigsaw A jigsaw will help you tackle intricate and curved cuts in timber or steel. Given that nothing in a van is straight, this is a must have tool!	
Mitre Saw A mitre saw will be used to cut most of your structural timber and shiplap. It's extremely easy to use and will save you a lot of time.	
Leveler A leveler will help you make sure your frames are angled correctly.	
Measuring Tape This is a good day to practice the "measure twice, cut once" principle.	
Sandpaper Block Used to smooth wood surfaces. We liked using sandpaper blocks better than traditional sandpaper.	

STEP-BY-STEP GUIDE

Step 1: Use structural timber to build the frame of your bed. In our case, we built two layers. Pictured here is the first layer. We separated it using plywood to make it easier to store things separately. Use plenty of angle brackets to make sure everything is solid.

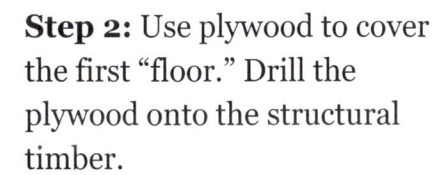

Step 2: Use plywood to cover the first "floor." Drill the plywood onto the structural timber.

Step 3: Make sure to have a way to access your electrical system. In our case, we've built a hatch so we can easily remove it if we need to access our electrical system or batteries.

Step 4: We used a rectangular piece of plywood for the hatch. We cut it with rounded corners using a Jigsaw, then drilled two holes in the middle to allow us to easily move it in and out. Make sure to sand the corners of the hatch and holes to avoid splinters.

Step 5: Place the hatch and make sure it fits perfectly.

Step 6: Build the second layer of your frame using structural wood and plywood.

Step 7: Along the side of our bed, we built a small cabinet. Half we use as a "night drawer" with a switch for lights and plugs for our phones. The other half is housing a laundry bag.

Day 17: Painting & Staining

Today will be a fun day! Painting and Staining.

We'll be staining the shiplap on the ceiling as we've decided to keep them "wood finish." For the walls and hanging cabinets, we'll be painting them white.

SUPPLIES NEEDED

Item	Qty	Picture
Plastic Tarp Used when painting.	2	
Primer & Paint We recommend using a primer & paint combo to save time. You'll likely need three coats of paint.	2	
Wood Stain We opted for oak finish wood stain. We strongly recommend finishing any exposed wood with wood stain. It makes it look 100 times better. You'll likely need three or more coats.	1	
Bitumen Waterproof Paint (optional) We decided to paint our under-the-bed storage area with bitumen waterproof paint because we store a lot of (sometimes wet) ocean-related equipment.	2	
Paint Brush Set Make sure to get a variety of paint brushes. You'll need small ones for finishes. Make sure you buy enough, as you'll end up needing more than you think. You may buy a paint roller as well to cover large surfaces faster.	1	

TOOLS NEEDED

Item	Picture
Sandpaper Block Used to smooth wood surfaces. We liked using sandpaper blocks better than traditional sandpaper.	
Painter's Tape This will be used to cover your edges before painting.	

STEP-BY-STEP GUIDE

Step 1: Sand your wood prior to staining and/or painting. We liked sandpaper blocks best, as they help you sand evenly and get into those weird corners.

Step 2: Carefully apply painter's tape where needed prior to painting. Use a tarp to cover your electrical system to avoid dripping paint or stain over it.

Step 3: Consider anywhere else you'd like to paint. We used bitumen waterproof paint in our storage area.

Day 18: Kitchen

Today, you'll be setting up the kitchen.

We opted for pre-built kitchen cabinets to save time and because it costs almost just as much to make them yourself.

In our kitchen, we have a large sink, a freezer/fridge, two large counter spaces, and a trash compartment. We have four cabinets.

SUPPLIES NEEDED

Item	Qty	Picture
Kitchen Cabinets - 3 Drawers We opted for the 450mm cabinets to house our kitchen utensils, pans, etc.	1	
Kitchen Cabinets - Base We opted for these 400mm base cabinets. One to house our sink and the other one for our trash.	2	
Kitchen Cabinets - Skinny Base We opted for this 200mm skinny base cabinet to go on the side of our fridge. This will be used for our toiletries.	1	
Kitchen Counters We opted for these 2200 x 600 x 26mm Acacia Solid Oiled Hardwood slabs for our counters. We stained them using wood stain and food safe protectant.	2	
Fridge / Freezer We opted for a 144L fridge / freezer. We went with the Vitrifrigo DRW180A because we want a large freezer to store our fish.	1	

Stove Burner We opted for a portable stove with 2 burners because it can easily be stored away and be used outside, which is where we prefer cooking.	1	
Sink We opted for a 37x44 cm Ikea sink because it fit perfectly on a 400mm cabinet and is big enough to be functional.	1	
Sink Mixer We opted for this sink mixer, hower we'd recommend getting a large one with a detachable hose as it makes doing dishes easier.	1	
2440x1220x6mm Structural Plywood This plywood will frame out the space for our fridge/freezer.	2	
Sikaflex Pro Make sure you buy it in whatever color your kitchen finishes are -- in our case white, or in clear.	2	
Timber screws Use 25mm to 45mm timber screws.	30	

Angle Brackets	5	
Use a variety of angle brackets to		
support your timber frames.		

TOOLS NEEDED

Item	Picture
Drill Big day for the drill -- be sure to have it (or them) charged up!	
Jigsaw You'll be using wood blades today.	
Holesaw Kit You'll be using wood bits today.	
Leveler A leveler will help you make sure your cabinets are angled correctly.	
Caulk Gun This low cost tool will help you distribute silicone, gap filler & adhesive cartridges easily.	

STEP-BY-STEP GUIDE

Step 1: Assemble the kitchen cabinets and place them in the kitchen. Notice that we had to drill a hole (using our jigsaw) to accommodate for our water heater. Make sure your cabinets are leveled. Adjust the legs if needed.

Step 2: Build an enclosure for your fridge (if needed) using plywood. Be sure to check measurements for the external portion of your fridge, as well as any holes you may need to cut for ventilation (this will likely be on the bottom / back / sides).

Step 3: Cut your countertop(s) using the jigsaw and file the edges smooth. Secure in place using angle brackets and / or Sikaflex.

Step 4: Set your sink in place. To cut this hole, measure the hole, drill a hole in one corner then use the jigsaw to cut along the path. Secure the sink using Sikaflex (clear is probably best). Set your sink mixer in place.

Step 5: We cut a hatch in our countertop and set up gas struts to it to build a trash compartment.

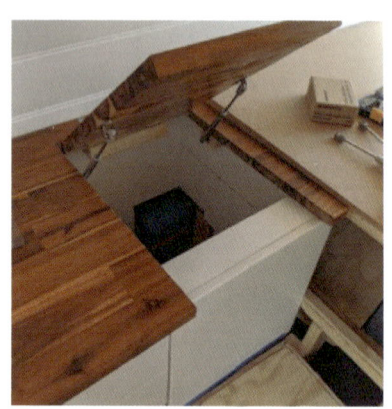

Day 19: Sofa

Today, we'll be building a small sofa.

First, we'll build the frame for it using structural timber. Then, we'll build cushions that act as a hatch. We like this solution because it allows you to store a huge amount of goods underneath the sofa and the cushion / hatch makes it really easy to access (and also comfy to sit on).

SUPPLIES NEEDED

Item	Qty	Picture
Structural Pine Timber: 35x75mmx2.4m You'll use this to frame your sofa.	10	
2440x1220x6mm Structural Plywood This will be the base of your cushions, and the outside of your sofa base.	2	
High-Density Foam These are not all created equal. Be sure to read about your options and select one that is intended for use as a cushion or something similar.	2	
Fabric We opted for matching grey fabric for our sofa and curtains.	1	
Timber Screws Use 25mm to 45mm timber screws.	100	
Angle Brackets Use a variety of angle brackets to support your timber frames.	30	

TOOLS NEEDED

Item	Picture
Drill Make sure to get a cordless drill. You'll actually really want to have two to avoid having to switch bits all the time.	
Jigsaw This will help you cut a "hatch" in your sofa.	
Mitre Saw This will cut your structural wood.	
Stapler Get either a manual stapler (cheaper) or a stapling gun (more fun). Today is the only day you'll use this tool for the build, so borrow if possible.	
Leveler A leveler will help you make sure you frames are angled correctly.	
Measuring tape Have you lost yours yet?	

Utility Knife
Used to cut your foam pads.

STEP-BY-STEP GUIDE

Step 1: Start building the frame of your sofa using structural timber. Use angle brackets to make sure everything is solid.

Step 2: Finish the rest of the frame.

Step 3: Use plywood for the sides and top covers. Then cut "hatches" using your jigsaw. In our case these were rounded rectangles just about 3cm smaller than the size of each top. No need to cut holes in them, as you'll be adding your cushions on top.

Step 4: Use each "hatch" to build a sofa cushion. Cut the high density foam using a utility knife (or kitchen knife). You'll want the foam cushion to be the size of the full top of each section of your couch, so slightly bigger than your hatch.

Step 5: Wrap your fabric and staple it onto the "hatch"

Step 6: Place the finished cushions/hatches and make sure they fit perfectly.

Step 7: That's it! Your sofa is ready to be enjoyed!

Day 20: Storage and Floors

Today, we'll be building the storage drawers for the back of our van, and installing our final flooring!

Building the storage drawers is a pretty easy step but make sure you measure twice. In our case, we had to redo the drawers three times because we incorrectly measured… maybe we were just tired after almost three weeks of non stop building.

Then, we'll set up the flooring. This is super easy.

SUPPLIES NEEDED

Item	Qty	Picture
2440x1220x6mm Structural Plywood This will be the sides of your drawers.	2	
Drawer Slides Use extra heavy drawer slides if you build long drawers.	2	
Door Handle To help you pull out your back storage drawers.	2	
Metal Hook (optional) We mounted these on our back storage drawers so we can hang towels, wetsuits, etc. while the van is open.	4	
Timber screws Use 25mm to 45mm timber screws.	100	
Angle Brackets Use a variety of angle brackets to support your timber frames.	30	

Self-Adhesive FlooringPlanks Super easy and durable option for your floors.	1	
Flooring Primer and Additive You need to brush primer and additive on your floor prior to glueing adhesive flooring.	1	
Aerosol Spray Adhesive (optional) Spray this on your floor just before glueing your adhesive floors. This will create an even stronger bond.	1	

TOOLS NEEDED

Item	Picture
Drill Hopefully you won't have to use the "reverse" function on yours as much as we did during this day of the build...	
Jigsaw You'll use this to cut your drawer sides.	
Measuring tape The measuring tape is the star of the day today.	
Utility Knife Used to cut your flooring to the correct shape and size.	

STEP-BY-STEP GUIDE: STORAGE DRAWERS

Step 1: Cut the bottom and each side of the drawers using a jigsaw. Assemble the drawer. We used angle brackets to make things easy.

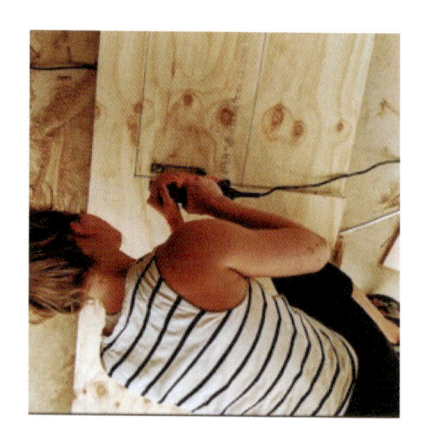

Step 2: Fix drawer slides to the bottom of your drawer slots, and to the drawers themselves. Slide the drawers in place. This may take some fiddling to get right. You'll definitely need a partner if you have long drawers.

Step 3: Add handles to the drawers. Later on, we also added little hooks so we can hang towels or wetsuits to dry.

STEP-BY-STEP GUIDE: FLOORING

Step 1: Starting on one side (ideally the side that you want to be most perfect), cut your adhesive flooring to the correct size, using a utility knife or kitchen scissors (we found scissors to be easier, but they're likely to get ruined by the end).

Step 2: Lay all of your pieces on the floor to ensure they fit nicely. Then, remove your pieces (lay them out in the right order outside of your van) and brush primer and additive on the full floor. Let it dry. You can also spray adhesive for extra hold.

Step 3: One at a time, remove the adhesive protector from the back of each piece of flooring and stick each in place.

Step 4: Place heavy objects (books or weights) on your floors for a few hours until they're dry.

Day 21: Finishes

Last day! Today, we will be completing all of the finishes.

You will likely have your own list of to-dos to make your van perfect, but below are most of the finishes we thought you might like to think about.

Ceiling finish: Once your wood stain is dry, pop in the lights. In addition, secure the fan cover in place using the provided screws.

Window covers: Cut a piece of cardboard to the correct shape of your window (this will take a lot of fiddling to get right). Glue your fabric to the inside half, and on the outside half use a reflective tape or sheet. Use velcro to secure the cardboard on the windows for easy removal.

Curtain: Again, using the same fabric, we cut a little curtain to close off the front of the van. We used a picture mounting wire from Ikea to hang this.

Grass Step: We bought a small piece of fake grass and covered the step with it. We used velcro to secure it so it's easy to remove and shake when it's covered in sand.

Aluminium Angle: We cut a small piece of aluminium angle to cover the edge of the step. It makes the floor look spectacular.

Kitchen rack: We added a towel rack with hooks, basket and fruit hammocks in the kitchen. All from Ikea. We love this setup.

Knife Holder: We added this magnetic knife holder from Ikea. Love it, too! Everything stays in place well even when we take rough roads.

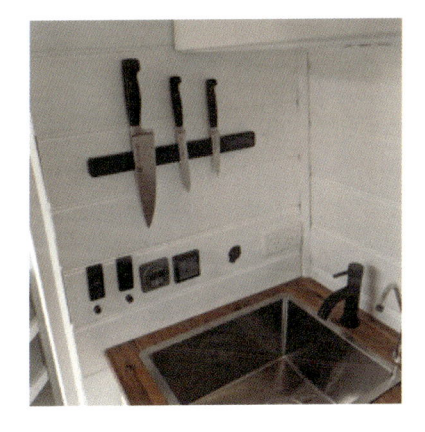

Kitchen drawer handles: We added leather handles (from Ikea) to our kitchen cabinets.

Hanging cabinets handles: We added leather handles (matching, from Ikea) to our hanging cabinets as well.

Drawer Pegs: When we started driving, we noticed that our kitchen drawers would not stay closed, despite our magnetic solution intended to keep them closed. After trying several systems, we drilled small holes from the sides of the drawers (inside the sink cabinet) and added small wooden pegs with hooks. We secure these in place before driving -- it takes all of 5 seconds.

Safety Equipment: We added a carbon monoxide detector, as well as a small fire extinguisher. Check your local regulations to see if you need to add anything else.

Spice Racks: We added these small spice racks from Ikea and painted them white. Thanks to the addition of small adhesive gel buttons from the hardware store, these never make a sound even as we drive on rough roads.

Shower Hooks: We added these small hooks to the side wall of the shower. We use them for our bath towels, bathing suits, hats, etc.

Shower Mat: We built this wood shower mat by glueing small pieces of wood then staining them with a waterproof solution. This helps cover up when our shower gets sand in it after a long day at the beach.

Mosquito nets: We bought mosquito nets from the hardware store and secured them on the door opening using velcro (one for our side door, and one for the back).

Part 5: Conclusion

LAST NOTE

We love Van Life and we absolutely adore our van. It is perfect for us. The layout, storage, showers, etc. fits our lifestyle perfectly.

We hope that, by reading and understanding all the steps involved in building our van, you will be able to customize the process to build YOUR dream home.

While this book is not exhaustive and you'll likely need to spend more time researching, we hope this book will help you make your dream come true... and maybe one day we will meet on the road!

ABOUT US

We're Georgia and Ben.

Georgia was born in Jefferson City, Missouri, USA, and moved to San Francisco after college. She worked in communications and public relations for several tech startups, investment firms, and nonprofits. Georgia loves cats, turtles, and eating chocolate. She enjoys freediving, hiking, and reading.

Ben was born in Nantes, France, and moved to Canada when he was 18 years old. After college, he started a tech start-up in Toronto then moved to San Francisco. He started a second tech start-up there and sold them both. He loves whales, sharks, and eating carrots. He enjoys kitesurfing, spearfishing, and hiking.

We met in San Francisco, and after a few years (and an underwater proposal) decided to leave our jobs and careers to live in a van full-time. We moved to Australia, where we built our first van. We're currently finishing our tour of the magic continent.

Follow our adventures on Instagram: TwoFishOutOfWater

Printed in Great Britain
by Amazon